Venner F. Milewski, Jr

Fighting Ships of the U.S. Navy 1883–2019

BATTLESHIPS AND "NEW NAVY" MONITORS

Volume TWO

STRATUS

Published in Poland in 2021
by STRATUS s.j.
Po. Box 123,
27-600 Sandomierz 1, Poland
e-mail: office@mmpbooks.biz
as
MMPBooks,
e-mail: rogerw@mmpbooks.biz

http://www.mmpbooks.biz

ISBN
978-83-66549-01-2

Editor in chief
Roger Wallsgrove

Editorial Team
Bartłomiej Belcarz
Robert Pęczkowski
Artur Juszczak

Text and research
Venner F. Milewski, Jr

Proofreading
Roger Wallsgrove

DTP
Stratus sp. j.

Printed by
Wydawnictwo
Diecezjalne i Drukarnia
w Sandomierzu
www.wds.pl

PRINTED IN POLAND

This series is dedicated to my father, Venner F. Milewski, Sr, for teaching me that there benefits to weathering the turbulent seas of life and to my son, Venner F. Milewski, III, my sounding-board, my co-pilot, my wingman, my mini-me and my greatest joy for teaching me more about myself and making me want to be a better person.

Acknowledgments

I need to show my appreciation to so many. During the four or more decades of research for this project, I have come in contact with countless people, most of which their names elude me. However, there are some people that have contributed significantly.

The late Samuel L. Morison was one of these people. He provided his assistance in developing the format, offering the use of his research material, and proofing the original manuscripts. Mr. A.D. Baker III so generously gave me permission to scan and use photographs from his extensive collection. He also collaborated on many technical aspects of the manuscript. JOC (SW/AW) Mark O. Piggott, U.S. Navy, Retired, worked years diligently proof-reading thousands of pages of manuscripts and thousands of photograph captions. Ray D. Bean provided many photographs from his considerable collection, especially, photographs of the elusive ships from foreign countries in the WWII Lend/Lease Program and Chris Wright for his technical assistance.

The Staffs of the Library of Congress and the Naval History and Heritage Command for their invaluable help for their many years of service in assisting me with ship histories, locating numerous books and patiently answering my many questions. The Mariners' Museum, Newport News, Virginia and Staff for assisting me, especially from Library Reference: Tom Moore, Jay Moore, Jennifer Anielski and Patty Hinson and from the Photographic Department: Claudia Jew, Megan Evans, Crystal Hines and Brock Switzer.

My friends, Lt. Col. PCN Dexter-Banks, Royal Marines Retired, MSgt Nelson Muñoz, USAF Retired and CTRCS(SW) Mark A. Guillory, USN Retired for taking your valuable time to read through the final copy of the manuscript and giving your honest, unfiltered opinions.

Venner F. Milewski, III, for providing endless 24 hour technical support, in addition to working thousands of hours selecting the photographs that appear in this series. You helped scan and organize over 24,000 photographs. Your attention to detail is unparalleled. Mostly, you are my informational sounding board and we share a passion for ships. I am so proud to call you, my son.

And finally, what can I say about my wife, Robin? You pushed me when I needed to be pushed. You encouraged me when I thought this was futile. You have been my rock. Thank you for all the proof reading, photograph selection parties, office supply runs, late nights, and un-fulfilled honey-do lists. Thank you for allowing me to continue this for the 33 years we have been married to see this to completion (without divorcing me). And yes, I will get right on cleaning that garage! I Love You.

Cover photo: Nevada BB-36 — Photograph taken, November 1915, while underway at high speed, making 22.5 knots during builder's sea trials off of Rockland, ME. (Ray D. Bean photo collection)

Unless otherwise noted, all photographs are courtesy of The Mariners' Museum, Newport News, Virginia

Table of Contents

Preface

From a very young age, I was in awe of ships, especially naval ships. I was intrigued by the aircraft carrier that looks so bare without her aircraft, the battleship with her huge guns and the destroyer with her speed and maneuverability.

At the start of my long naval career, I decided to work on a book about U.S. Naval Warships. The data in it would be from as many official government sources as were available. After many decades of in-depth research, different formats, data additions and the countless duty station changes, I finally arrived at what I originally started out to do. However, with the addition of such a large amount of photographs, it now became apparent that one book would never hold everything. It would have to be a series.

Each book in the series contains in-depth information to include: dates for contracts, launches, commissionings, and so much more. There is a synopsis of her history. "As built" class specifications tables are included along with the tables for those ships that went through major overhauls. I have tried to include photographs showing profiles of the many different ships in their various camouflage patterns throughout their naval career.

Whether you are a researcher, naval historian, ship modeler, sailor (or someone who loves a sailor), or just someone interested in learning more about U.S. Naval Warships, I am sure that you will find this series of books to be the most complete and comprehensive available anywhere.

Glossary of Terms and Abbreviations

A. Ship Classifications	
AB	Crane Ship
ACR	Armored Cruiser
AG	Miscellaneous Auxiliary
BB	Battleship
BM	Monitor
CV	Aircraft Carrier
IX	Unclassified

B. Shipbuilding and Conversion Companies and Yards	
Bath Iron	Bath Iron Works, Bath, ME.
Beth., Quincy	Bethlehem Steel Co., Shipbuilding Division, Quincy, MA.
Beth., Ship	Bethlehem Shipbuilding Corp., Quincy, MA.
Fore R S & E	Fore River Ship & Engine Co., Fore River, MA.
Fore River	Fore River Shipbuilding Co., Quincy, MA.
Harlan	Harlan & Hollingsworth Co., Wilmington, DE.
John Roach	John Roach & Sons, Chester, PA.
Lewis Nixon	Lewis Nixon & The Crescent Shipyard, Elizabethport, NJ.
Mare I.	Mare Island Navy Yard, Vallejo, CA.
Moran Bros.	Moran Brothers, Seattle, WA.
NNS&DD Co.	Newport News Shipbuilding & Dry Dock Co., Newport News, VA.
NY Ship Co.	New York Shipbuilding Co., Camden, NJ.
NY Ship Corp.	New York Shipbuilding Corp., Camden, NJ.
New York NY	New York Navy Yard, Brooklyn, NY.
Norfolk NY	Norfolk Navy Yard, Portsmouth, VA.
Phil., NY	Philadelphia Navy Yard, Philadelphia, PA.
Phineas	Phineas Burgess & The Continental Iron Works, Vallejo, CA.
Union Iron	Union Iron Works, San Francisco, CA.
W. Cramp	William Cramp & Sons, Ship & Engine Building Co., Philadelphia, PA.

C. Machinery Manufacturers	
B & W	Babcock & Wilcox Co., Boiler Division, Barberton, OH.
Bath	Bath Iron Works, Bath, ME.
Bureau Express	Information Needed
Continental Iron	Phineas Burgess & The Continental Iron Works, Vallejo, CA.
Cramp	William Cramp & Sons, Ship & Engine Building Co., Philadelphia, PA.
Curtis	Curtis type turbine manufactured by the following: Fore River Shipbuilding Co., Quincy, MA.
Fore R S & E	Fore River Ship & Engine Building Co., Fore River, MA.
Foster-Wheeler	Foster-Wheeler Corp., Mountaintop, PA.
General Electric	General Electric Co., Schenectady, NY.
Harlan & Hollingsworth	Harlan & Hollingsworth Corp., Wilmington, DE.
John Roach	John Roach & Sons, Chester, PA.
Lewis Nixon	Lewis Nixon & The Crescent Shipyard, Elizabethport, NJ.
Moran	Moran Brothers Co., Seattle, WA.
Mosher	Mosher type boiler manufactured by the following: Fore River Shipbuilding Co., Quincy, MA. Lewis Nixon & The Crescent Shipyard, Elizabethport, NJ. Newport News Shipbuilding & Dry Dock Co., Newport News, VA.

New York NY	New York Navy Yard, Brooklyn, NY.
NY Ship Co.	New York Shipbuilding Co., Camden, NJ.
Newport News	Newport News Shipbuilding & Dry Dock Co., Newport News, VA.
Niclausse	Niclausse type boiler built by the Stirling Co., Barberton, OH.
Norfolk Navy Yard	Norfolk Navy Yard, Portsmouth, VA.
Parsons	Parsons type turbine manufactured by the following: New York Shipbuilding Co., Camden, NJ. New York Shipbuilding Corp., Camden, NJ. William Cramp & Sons, Ship & Engine Building Co., Philadelphia, PA.
Quintard Iron Wks	Quintard Iron Works, New York City, NY.
Richmond Loco. Wks	Richmond Locomotive Works, Richmond, VA.
Thornycroft	Thornycroft type boiler manufactured by the following: Newport News Shipbuilding & Dry Dock Co., Newport News, VA Union Iron Works, San Francisco, CA.
Union	Union Iron Works, San Francisco, CA.
Westinghouse	Westinghouse Electric Co., Pittsburgh, PA.
White-Forster	White-Forster type boiler built by the Babcock & Wilcox Co., Barberton, OH.
Yarrow	Yarrow type boiler manufactured by the following: Bethlehem Shipbuilding Corp., Quincy, MA Fore River Shipbuilding Co., Quincy, MA.

D. Miscellaneous Abbreviations	
AA	Antiaircraft
B.L.R.	Breach Loading Rifle
Bros.	Brothers
cal.	caliber
CAPT	Captain
CDR	Commander
CIWS	Close-In Weapons System
Co.	Company
Comm.	Commission
Corp.	Corporation
Decomm.	Decommission
Div.	Division
DP	Dual Purpose (surface & anti-air)
FT (Scotch)	Fire Tube (Scotch-type) Boiler
FY	Fiscal Year
H.R.C.	Hotchkiss Revolving Cannon
Inc.	Incorporated
Ltd.	Limited
mg.	machine gun
mm	millimeter
No.	Number
NVR	Naval Vessels Register
pdr.	pounder
quad.	quadruple
R.F.	Rapid Fire
Recip.	Reciprocation
Reclass.	Reclassified
Recomm.	Recommission
SSM	Surface-to-Surface Missile
TASM	Tomahawk Anti Ship Missile
TD	Turbine Direct
TDD	Turbine Direct Drive
TED	Turbine Electric Drive
TLAM	Tomahawk Land Attack Missile
TRD	Turbine Reduction Drive

Trans.	Transfer or Transferred
USS	United States Ship
Vert.	Vertical
WT	Water Tube Boiler
3-Exp.	Triple Expansion

E.Symbols

" " Used to identify vessels, although shown with an official hull classification, did not receive that classification due to being stricken from the Naval Vessels Register prior to 7/17/20. The symbol appears in the Battleship, Destroyer and Submarine sections.

Battleships

1. MAINE CLASS (BB)

Maine (BB)

NAME (HULL NO.)	BUILDER	KEEL LAID	LAUNCHED	COMMISSIONED
MAINE BB	New York NY	17 Oct 1888	18 Nov 1890	17 Sep 1895

Authorized 3 Aug 1886. Sponsored by Miss Alice T. Wilmerding. First Commanding Officer: CAPT Alton S. Crowninshield. Originally rated as ARMORED CRUISER NO. 1. Rerated as a Second-Class BB on 17 Sep 1895. Sunk 15 Feb 1898 in the harbor of Havana, Cuba, at 9:40 PM, by an underwater explosion that set off the forward magazine. Hulk raised 2 Feb 1912 and towed out into the Gulf of Mexico. Sunk 16 Mar 1912, by scuttling, with appropriate ceremonies and honors.

Maine BB — Photograph taken, between her launching on 18 November 1890 and commissioning 17 September 1895, coming off a very successful sea trial. Note the broom attached to the forward mast (meaning "Clean Sweep" at Sea Trials) and the 18.2 (knots) painted on the forward stack. Also note that her port side main armament had not yet been installed.

Maine BB — Photograph taken, 18 June 1911, looking forward showing some of the ship during the process of pumping out the water from the cofferdam. Note the forward superstructure lying upside down on the aft part of the wreck.

Class Specifications			As Completed (1895)
HULL	LENGTH	Waterline	318' 3"
		Overall	324' 4"
	EXTREME BEAM		57' 2"
	DISPLACEMENT	Full Load	6,843 tons
		Normal	6.020 tons
	MAXIMUM DRAFT		22' 11"
	COMPLEMENT	Officers	31
		Enlisted	343
ARMAMENT		Main	(2) twin 10" B.L.R. turrets
		Secondary	(6) single 6" B.L.R. mounts
			(7) single 6 pdr. R.F.
			(4) single 1 pdr. R.F.
			(4) gatling mg.
		Torpedo Tubes	(6) 18" surface
	ARMOR	Belt	12" at waterline
		Bulkheads	6"
		Deck	2"
		Turrets	8"
		Barbettes	12"
		Conning Tower	10"
ENGINEERING	SPEED	Maximum	17.4 knots
		Economical	10.0 knots
	ENGINES	Manufacturer	Quintard Iron Wks
		Type	Vert. 3-Exp. Recip.
	HORSEPOWER	Indicated	9,171
	SCREWS		2
	BOILERS	Manufacturer	Quintard Iron Wks
		Type/No.	FT (Scotch)/4
	FUEL CAPACITY		896 tons coal

2: TEXAS CLASS (BB)

Texas (BB)

NAME (HULL NO.)	BUILDER	KEEL LAID	LAUNCHED	COMMISSIONED
TEXAS BB	Norfolk NY	1 Jun 1889	28 Jun 1892	15 Aug 1895

Authorized 3 Aug 1886. Sponsored by Miss Madge M. Williams. First Commanding Officer: CAPT Henry Glass. Rated as Second-Class BB. Decomm. 27 Jan 1896 at Norfolk, VA. Recomm 20 Jul 1896. Decomm. 3 Nov 1900 at Norfolk, VA. Recomm. 3 Nov 1902. Placed in comm., in reserve, 24 May 1906 at Norfolk, VA. Placed in full comm. 29 Sep 1906. Placed in comm., in reserve, 9 Nov 1906 at Norfolk, VA. Decomm. 11 Jan 1908 at Norfolk, VA. Recomm. 1 Sep 1908. Decomm. 11 Feb 1911 at Norfolk, VA. Renamed SAN MARCOS 16 Feb 1911. Sunk 11 Mar 1911, as a target, in shallow water, by naval gunfire seven miles south-southwest off the southern tip of Tangier Island, MD. Struck 11 Oct 1911 from the NVR. Due to several ships striking the sunken hulk, all parts of the wreck projecting above the water were destroyed in 1944.

Texas BB — Photograph taken, 1898, at New York City, NY, probably upon her return from the Spanish-American War. (U.S. Naval History and Heritage Command Photo)

San Marcos BB — Photograph taken, March 1911, anchored in Tangier Sound in Chesapeake Bay, MD, prior to being used as a target in ordnance tests by USS New Hampshire (BB-25). Note that the old battleship had canvas screens rigged to increase the target area. (U.S. Naval History and Heritage Command Photo)

San Marcos BB — Photograph taken, March 1911, anchored in Tangier Sound in Chesapeake Bay, VA. Naval personnel were inspecting the damage to the ship's superstructure, following her being used as a target by USS New Hampshire (BB-25). (U.S. Naval History and Heritage Command Photo)

Class Specifications			As Completed (1895)
HULL	LENGTH	Waterline	301' 4"
		Overall	308' 10"
	EXTREME BEAM		64' 1"
	DISPLACEMENT	Full Load	6,770 tons
		Normal	6,327 tons
	MAXIMUM DRAFT		25' 3"
	COMPLEMENT	Officers	30
		Enlisted	362
ARMAMENT		Main	(2) single 12"/35 B.L.R. turrets
		Secondary	(6) single 6"/35 B.L.R. mounts
			(12) 6 pdr. R.F.
			(6) 1 pdr. R.F.
			(4) 37 mm. H.R.C. cylindrical
			(2) gatling mg.
		Torpedo Tubes	(4) 14" surface
	ARMOR	Belt	12" at waterline
		Bulkheads	6"
		Deck	2" – 3"
		Turrets	12"
		Barbettes	12"
		Conning Tower	12"
ENGINEERING	SPEED	Maximum	17.0 knots
		Economical	11.8 knots
	ENGINES	Manufacturer	Richmond Loco. Wks
		Type	Vert. 3-Exp. Recip.
	HORSEPOWER	Indicated	8,610
	SCREWS		2
	BOILERS	Manufacturer	Norfolk Navy Yard
		Type/No.	Double-ended, cylindrical
			FT (Scotch)/4
	FUEL CAPACITY		850 tons coal

3: INDIANA CLASS (BB-1 to BB-3)

Indiana "(BB-1)"

NAME (HULL NO.)	BUILDER	KEEL LAID	LAUNCHED	COMMISSIONED
INDIANA "(BB-1)"	W. Cramp	7 May 1891	28 Feb 1893	20 Nov 1895

Authorized 30 Jun 1890. Contract awarded 19 Nov 1890. Sponsored by Miss Jessie Miller. First Commanding Officer: CAPT Robley D. Evans. Rated as COAST BATTLESHIP NO. 1. Decomm. 29 Dec 1903 at Brooklyn, NY. Recomm. 8 Jan 1906. Placed in comm., in reserve, 19 Jul 1907 at Philadelphia, PA. Placed in full comm. 10 May 1910. Placed in comm., in reserve, 13 Sep 1910 at Philadelphia, PA. Placed in full comm. 3 May 1911. Placed in comm., in reserve, 1 Sep 1911 at Philadelphia, PA. Decomm. 23 May 1914 at Philadelphia, PA. Recomm. 9 Jun 1917. Name cancelled 29 Mar 1919. Renamed COAST BATTLESHIP NO. 1 on 29 Mar 1919. Decomm. 31 Mar 1919 at Philadelphia, PA. Struck 6 Nov 1919 from the NVR. Never assigned hull number BB-1. Would have been, had INDIANA still been on the NVR. Sunk 1 Nov 1920 as a bombing target off Tangier Island, MD. Hulk sold 19 Mar 1924 for scrap to the Steel Scrap Co., Philadelphia, PA, for $92,969.76.

Indiana BB-1 — Photograph taken, summer 1898, anchored at New York City, NY. Note the six-pounder broadside battery on the upper deck amidships and just aft of the bridge, and the one-pounders in the foremast fighting tops. USS Iowa (BB-4) is in back of the USS Indiana.

Indiana BB-1 — Photograph taken, circa 1900, while underway at an unknown location. (Official U.S. Navy Photo)

Indiana BB-1 — Photograph taken, 1 April 1910, in drydock showing the Lacoste Ship Brake. The brake was designed to stop ships in the event of impending collisions. The results were inconclusive.

Massachusetts (BB-2)

NAME (HULL NO.)	BUILDER	KEEL LAID	LAUNCHED	COMMISSIONED
MASSACHUSETTS (BB-2)	W. Cramp	25 Jun 1891	10 Jun 1893	10 Jun 1896

Authorized 30 Jun 1890. Contract awarded 18 Nov 1890. Sponsored by Miss Leila Herbert. First Commanding Officer: CAPT Frederick Rodgers. Rated as COAST BATTLESHIP NO. 2. Decomm. 8 Jan 1906 at Brooklyn, NY. Recomm. 28 Apr 1910. Placed in comm., in reserve, 1 Sep 1910 at Philadelphia, PA. Placed in full comm. 3 May 1911. Placed in comm., in reserve, 1 Sep 1911 at Philadelphia, PA. Placed in full comm. 4 Jun 1912. Placed in comm., in reserve, 2 Sep 1912 at Philadelphia, PA. Decomm. 23 May 1914 at Philadelphia, PA. Recomm. 6 May 1917. Name cancelled 29 Mar 1919. Renamed COAST BATTLESHIP NO. 2 on 29 Mar 1919. Decomm. 31 Mar 1919 at Philadelphia, PA. Classified BB-2 on 17 Jul 1920. Struck 22 Nov 1920 from the NVR and trans. to the War Department the same date. Scuttled 6 Jan 1921 off Pensacola Bar, FL, for use as a target ship by artillery batteries from Fort Pickens, Pensacola, FL. Returned 20 Feb 1925 to the Navy for sale as scrap. Declared to be the property of the State of Florida 15 Nov 1956. Hulk still rests two miles Southwest of Pensacola Bay resting in 20–30 feet of water. Parts of her superstructure are exposed.

Massachusetts BB-2 — Photograph taken, summer 1896, during shakedown off the East Coast of the United States.

Massachusetts BB-2 — Photograph taken, July 1910, anchored at Marseille, France. (U.S. Naval History and Heritage Command Photo)

NAME (HULL NO.)	BUILDER	KEEL LAID	LAUNCHED	COMMISSIONED
OREGON (BB-3)	Union Iron	19 Nov 1891	26 Oct 1893	15 Jul 1896

Authorized 30 Jun 1890. Contract awarded 19 Nov 1890. Sponsored by Miss Daisy Ainsworth. First Commanding Officer: CAPT Henry L. Howison. Rated as COAST BATTLESHIP NO. 3. Decomm. 27 Apr 1906 at Bremerton, WA. Placed in comm., in reserve, 29 Aug 1911. Placed in full comm. 2 Jan 1915. Placed in comm., in reserve, 11 Feb 1916 at San Francisco, CA. Placed in full comm. 7 Apr 1917. Decomm. 12 Jun 1919 at Bremerton, WA. Recomm. 21 Aug 1919. Decomm. 4 Oct 1919 at Bremerton, WA. Classified BB-3 on 17 Jul 1920. Demilitarization completed by 4 Jan 1924 in accordance with the Washington Treaty for Naval Limitations. Reclass. UNCLASSIFIED VESSEL. Loaned to the State of Oregon as a floating memorial and museum 25 Jun 1925. Reclass. IX-22 on 17 Feb 1941. Struck 2 Nov 1942 from the NVR. Sold 7 Dec 1942 for scrapping to W. O. McKay Co., Seattle, WA. Reacquired September 1943 by the Navy. July-August 1944, towed to Guam for use as an explosives storage hulk. Sold 15 Mar 1956 for scrapping to the Massey Supply Corp., Kansas City, MO, for $208,000.00. Resold 1956 to Iwai Sanggo Co., Ltd., Kawasaki, Japan. Scrapped.

Oregon BB-3 — Photograph taken, 1898, while underway at an unknown location. (Official U.S. Navy Photo)

Oregon BB-3 — Photograph taken July-October 1898, in drydock during an overhaul by the New York Navy Yard, Brooklyn, NY. (Official U.S. Navy Photo)

Oregon BB-3 — Photograph taken 1913, anchored at an unknown location along the West Coast of the United States. (Ray D. Bean photo collection)

Class Specifications			As Completed (1895/1896)	Operational Condition as of 1916
HULL	LENGTH	Waterline	348’ 0”	348’ 0”
		Overall	350’ 11” (BB-1, 2)	350’ 11” (BB-1, 2)
			351’ 2” (BB-3)	351’ 2” (BB-3)
	EXTREME BEAM		69’ 3”	69’ 3”
	DISPLACEMENT	Full Load	11,403 tons	11,688 tons
		Normal	10,288 tons	10,288 tons
	MAXIMUM DRAFT		27’ 2”	27’ 2”
	COMPLEMENT	Officers	32	40
		Enlisted	411	647 (BB-1, 2)
				644 (BB-3)
		Marines	None	56
ARMAMENT		Main	(2) twin 13”/35 B.L.R. turrets	(2) twin 13”/35 B.L.R. turrets
			(4) twin 8”/35 B.L.R. turrets	(4) twin 8”/35 B.L.R. turrets
		Secondary	(4) single 6”/40 B.L.R. mounts	(12) single 3”/50 R.F. mounts
			(20) single 6 pdr.	(4) single 6 pdr., saluting
			(6) single 1 pdr.	
			(4) gatling mg.	
		Torpedo Tubes	(4) 18” surface (BB-1)	None
			(5) 18” surface (BB-2, 3)	
	ARMOR	Belt		
		Top	18”	18”
		Bottom	8.5”	8.5”
		Waterline	18”	18”
		Bulkheads	14”	14”
		Deck		
		Forward	3”	3”
		Aft	3”	3”
		Amidships	2.75”	2.75”
		13” Gun Turrets	15”	15”
		8” Gun Turrets	6”	6”
		13” Gun Barbettes	17”	17”
		8” Gun Barbettes	6” – 8”	6” – 8”
		Conning Tower	10”	10”
ENGINEERING	SPEED	Maximum	15.5 knots (BB-1)	15.5 knots (BB-1)
			16.2 knots (BB-2)	16.2 knots (BB-2)
			16.8 knots (BB-3)	16.8 knots (BB-3)
		Economical	10.0 knots	10.0 knots
	ENGINES	Manufacturer	Cramp (BB-1, 2)	Cramp (BB-1, 2)
			Union (BB-3)	Union (BB-3)
		Type	Vert. 3-Exp. Recip.	Vert. 3-Exp. Recip.
	HORSEPOWER	Indicated	9,738 (BB-1)	9,738 (BB-1)
			10,403 (BB-2)	10,403 (BB-2)
			11,111 (BB-3)	11,111 (BB-3)
	SCREWS		2	2
	BOILERS	Manufacturer	Cramp (BB-1, 2)	B & W (BB-1, 2)
			Union (BB-3)	Union (BB-3)
		Type/No.	Double-ended, cylindrical	WT/8 (BB-1, 2)
			FT (Scotch)/6	Double-ended, cylindrical
				FT (Scotch)/6
	FUEL CAPACITY		1,597 tons coal (BB-1, 2)	1,500 tons coal (BB-1)
			1,594 tons coal (BB-3)	1,487 tons coal (BB-2)
				1,425 tons coal (BB-3)

4: IOWA CLASS (BB-4)

Iowa (BB-4)

NAME (HULL NO.)	BUILDER	KEEL LAID	LAUNCHED	COMMISSIONED
IOWA (BB-4)	W. Cramp	5 Aug 1893	28 Mar 1896	16 Jun 1897

Authorized 19 Jul 1892. Contract awarded 11 Feb 1893. Sponsored by Miss Mary L. Drake. First Commanding Officer: CAPT William T. Sampson. Rated as COAST BATTLESHIP NO. 4. Decomm. 30 Jun 1903 at Brooklyn, NY. Recomm. 23 Dec 1903. Placed in comm., in reserve, 6 Jun 1907 at Norfolk, VA. Decomm. 23 Jul 1908 at Norfolk, VA. Recomm. 2 May 1910. Placed in comm., in reserve, 26 Sep 1910 at Philadelphia, PA. Placed in full comm. 3 May 1911. Placed in comm., in reserve, 1 Sep 1911 at Philadelphia, PA. Decomm. 23 May 1914 at Philadelphia, PA. Placed in limited comm. 23 Apr 1917 for service as receiving ship. Name cancelled 29 Mar 1919. Renamed COAST BATTLESHIP NO. 4 on 29 Mar 1919. Decomm. 31 Mar 1919 at Philadelphia, PA. Classified BB-4 on 17 Jul 1920. Reclass. UNCLASSIFIED VESSEL 1920 and employed as a radio controlled target. Reclass. IX-6 on 21 Jul 1921. Struck 27 Mar 1923 from the NVR. Sunk 22 Mar 1923 as a target by naval gunfire in Panama Bay, Canal Zone.

Iowa BB-4 — Photograph taken, 20 August 1898, anchored in New York Harbor, NY. (Ray D. Bean photo collection)

Iowa BB-4 — Photograph taken, circa 1911, anchored in New York Harbor, NY. (U.S. Naval History and Heritage Command Photo)

Iowa BB-4 — Photograph taken, 21 March 1923, while maneuvering under fire from USS Mississippi (BB-41), while being used as a radio-controlled target during fleet gunnery practice in the Gulf of Panama. Note the projectiles hitting the water on either side of the target. (U.S. Naval History and Heritage Command Photo)

Class Specifications			As Completed (1897)	Operational Condition as of 1919
HULL	LENGTH	Waterline	360' 0"	348' 0"
		Overall	362' 5"	362' 5"
	EXTREME BEAM		72' 3"	69' 3"
	DISPLACEMENT	Full Load	12,647 tons	11,688 tons
		Normal	11,346 tons	10,288 tons
	MAXIMUM DRAFT		26' 10"	26' 5"
	COMPLEMENT	Officers	36	42
		Enlisted	450	685
ARMAMENT		Main	(2) twin 12"/35 B.L.R. turrets	(2) twin 12"/35 B.L.R. turrets
			(4) twin 8"/35 B.L.R. turrets	(4) twin 8"/35 B.L.R. turrets
		Secondary	(6) single 4"/40 mounts	None
			(20) single 6 pdr.	
			(4) single 1 pdr.	
			(4) gatling mg.	
		Torpedo Tubes	(4) 14" surface	None
	ARMOR	Belt		
		Top	14"	14"
		Bottom	7"	7"
		Waterline	14"	14"
		Bulkheads	12"	12"
		Deck		
		Forward	3"	3"
		Aft	3"	3"
		Amidships	2.75"	2.75"
		12" Gun Turrets	15"	15" – 17"
		8" Gun Turrets	7" – 8"	7" – 8"
		12" Gun Barbettes	15"	12.5" – 15"
		8" Gun Barbettes	6" – 8"	6" – 8"
		Conning Tower	10"	10"
ENGINEERING	SPEED	Maximum	17.1 knots	17.1 knots
		Economical	10.0 knots	10.0 knots
	ENGINES	Manufacturer	Cramp	Cramp
		Type	Vert. 3-Exp. Recip.	Vert. 3-Exp. Recip.
	HORSEPOWER	Indicated	12,105	12,105
	SCREWS		2	2
	BOILERS	Manufacturer	Cramp	Cramp
		Type/No.	Double-ended, cylindrical	Double-ended, cylindrical
			FT (Scotch)/3	FT (Scotch)/3
			Single-ended, cylindrical	Single-ended, cylindrical
			FT (Scotch)/2	FT (Scotch)/2
	FUEL CAPACITY		1,650 tons coal	1,682 tons coal

5: KEARSARGE CLASS (BB-5 to BB-6)

Kearsarge (BB-5)

NAME (HULL NO.)	BUILDER	KEEL LAID	LAUNCHED	COMMISSIONED
KEARSARGE (BB-5)	NNS&DD Co.	30 Jun 1896	24 Mar 1898	20 Feb 1900

Authorized 2 Mar 1895. Contract awarded 2 Jan 1896. Sponsored by Mrs. Herbert Winslow. First Commanding Officer: CAPT William M. Folger. Rated as COAST BATTLESHIP NO. 5. Placed in comm., in reserve, 31 Mar 1909 at Philadelphia, PA. Decomm. 4 Sep 1909 at Philadelphia, PA. Placed in comm., in reserve, 17 Jun 1912. Placed in full comm. 23 Jun 1915. Decomm. 18 May 1920 at Philadelphia, PA. Classified BB-5 on 17 Jul 1920. Reclass. AB-1 on 5 Aug 1920. Renamed CRANE SHIP NO. 1 on 6 Nov 1941 when her name was assigned to CV-33. Struck 22 Jun 1955 from the NVR. Sold 9 Aug 1955 to the Patapsco Scrap Co., Baltimore, MD. Scrapped.

Kearsarge BB-5 — Photograph taken, September 1899, in drydock at the Newport News Shipbuilding & Dry Dock Co., Newport News, VA. Note that she was about five months away from her commissioning. (Official U.S. Navy Photo)

Kearsarge BB-5 — Photograph taken, circa 1903, tied up to a pier at an unknown location. Note her name in large letters around the bridge. (Official U.S. Navy Photo)

Kearsarge BB-5 — Photograph taken, February 1909, anchored in Hampton Roads, VA, after having returned from a world cruise. Note the ship was in full dress configuration. (Ray D. Bean photo collection)

Crane Ship No. 1 — Photograph taken, 14 May 1944, while underway in the Atlantic Ocean.

Kentucky (BB-6)

NAME (HULL NO.)	BUILDER	KEEL LAID	LAUNCHED	COMMISSIONED
KENTUCKY (BB-6)	NNS&DD Co.	30 Jun 1896	24 Mar 1898	15 May 1900

Authorized 2 Mar 1895. Contract awarded 2 Jan 1896. Sponsored by Miss Christine Bradley. First Commanding Officer: CAPT Colby H. Chester. Rated as COAST BATTLESHIP NO. 6. Placed in comm., in reserve, 12 Apr 1909 at Philadelphia, PA. Decomm. 28 Aug 1909 at Norfolk, VA. Placed in comm., in reserve, 4 Jun 1912. Placed in full comm. 23 Jun 1915. Decomm. 29 May 1920 at Philadelphia, PA. Classified BB-6 on 17 Jul 1920. Conversion to CRANE SHIP NO. 2 projected but cancelled. Struck 27 May 1922 from the NVR. Sold 24 Mar 1923 to the Dravo Construction Co., Pittsburgh, PA, for $103,500.00. Scrapped.

Kentucky BB-6 — Photograph taken, 31 May 1900, anchored in New York Harbor, NY, just after commissioning. Note the crews' laundry hanging from the lines to dry.

Kentucky BB-6 — Photograph taken, 1907, anchored at an unknown location along the East Coast of the United States. Note that she had been repainted with buff color above the first superstructure deck and white below that level. (Official U.S. Navy Photo)

Kentucky BB-6 — Photograph taken, 27 January 1920, at an unknown location along the East Coast of the United States. Note that most of her main deck 5" guns had been removed, leaving only those in the corners. This was done in order to provide additional berthing for troops coming back after the war. (Official U.S. Navy Photo)

Class Specifications			As Completed (1900)	Operational Condition as of 1919
HULL	LENGTH	Waterline	368' 0"	368' 0"
		Overall	375' 4"	375' 4"
	EXTREME BEAM		72' 3"	72' 2.5"
	DISPLACEMENT	Full Load	12,905 tons	12,320 tons
		Normal	11,540 tons	11,520 tons
	MAXIMUM DRAFT		25' 10"	
	COMPLEMENT	Officers	38 (BB-5), 40 (BB-6)	52
		Enlisted	548 (BB-5), 549 (BB-6)	815
ARMAMENT		Main	(2) twin 13"/35 B.L.R. turrets	(2) twin 13"/35 B.L.R. turrets
			(2) twin 8"/35 B.L.R. turrets	(2) twin 8"/35 B.L.R. turrets
		Secondary	(14) single 5"/40 mounts	(8) single 5"/40 mounts
			(20) single 6 pdr.	(2) single 3"/50 mounts
			(19) single 1 pdr.	(2) single 6 pdr. saluting
			(2) colt mg.	
	Torpedo Tubes		(4) 18" surface	None
	ARMOR	Belt		
		Top	16.5"	16.5"
		Bottom	9.5"	9.5"
		Waterline	13.75"	13.4"
		Bulkheads	10"– 12"	10"– 12"
		Deck		
		Forward	2.75" – 3"	2.75" – 3"
		Aft	2.75" – 5"	2.75" – 5"
		Amidships	2.75"	2.75"
		13" Gun Turrets	15" – 17"	15" – 17"
		8" Gun Turrets	9" – 11"	9" – 11"
		Barbettes	12" – 15"	12.6" – 15"
		Conning Tower	10"	10"
ENGINEERING	SPEED	Maximum	16.8 knots (BB-5)	16.8 knots (BB-5)
			16.9 knots (BB-6)	16.9 knots (BB-6)
		Economical	10.0 knots	10.0 knots
	ENGINES	Manufacturer	Newport News	Newport News
		Type	Vert. 3-Exp. Recip.	Vert. 3-Exp. Recip.
	HORSEPOWER	Indicated	11,788 (BB-5)	11,788 (BB-5)
			12,318 (BB-6)	12,318 (BB-6)
	SCREWS		2	2
	BOILERS	Manufacturer	Newport News	Mosher
		Type/No.	FT (Scotch)/5	WT/8
	FUEL CAPACITY		1,591 tons coal	1,679 tons coal (BB-5)
				1,658 tons coal (BB-6)

6: ILLINOIS CLASS (BB-7 to BB-9)

Illinois (BB-7)

NAME (HULL NO.)	BUILDER	KEEL LAID	LAUNCHED	COMMISSIONED
ILLINOIS (BB-7)	NNS&DD Co.	10 Feb 1897	4 Oct 1998	16 Sep 1901

Authorized 10 Jun 1896. Contract awarded 26 Sep 1896. Sponsored by Miss Nancy Leiter. First Commanding Officer: CAPT George A. Converse. Rated as COAST BATTLESHIP NO. 7. Placed in comm., in reserve, 1 Apr 1909 at Philadelphia, PA. Decomm. 4 Aug 1909 at Boston, MA. Placed in comm., in reserve, 15 Apr 1912. Placed in full comm. 2 Nov 1912. Placed in comm., in reserve, 16 Dec 1912 at Boston, MA. Placed in full comm. 1 Apr 1913. Placed in comm., in reserve, 5 Sep 1913 at Philadelphia, PA. Placed in full comm. 16 Mar 1914. Placed in comm., in reserve, 2 Dec 1914 at Philadelphia, PA. Decomm. 15 May 1920 at Philadelphia, PA. Classified BB-7 on 17 Jul 1920. Loaned 25 Oct 1921 to the New York Naval Militia as a training ship. Demilitarization completed by 14 Feb 1924 in accordance with the terms of the Washington Treaty for Naval Limitations. Reclass. UNCLASSIFIED VESSEL 1924. Renamed PRAIRE STATE 23 Jan 1941. Reclass. IX-15 on 17 Feb 1941. Struck 26 Mar 1956 from the NVR. Sold 18 May 1956 to the Bethlehem Steel Co., Bethlehem, PA, for $278,260.00. Scrapped.

Illinois BB-7 — Photograph taken, 6 January 1902, in drydock at the New Orleans Naval Station, Algiers, LA. At the time of the photograph, she was being used to test out a new floating drydock. (Ray D. Bean photo collection)

Illinois BB-7 — Photograph taken, circa 1901, anchored in an unknown harbor along the East Coast of the United States. (Official U.S. Navy Photo)

Illinois BB-7 — Photograph taken, 7 September 1914, underway at an unknown location during her summer Midshipmen training cruise to Europe.

Alabama (BB-8)

NAME (HULL NO.)	BUILDER	KEEL LAID	LAUNCHED	COMMISSIONED
ALABAMA (BB-8)	W. Cramp	1 Dec 1896	18 May 1898	16 Oct 1900

Authorized 10 Jun 1896. Contract awarded 24 Sep 1896. Sponsored by Miss Mary Morgan. First Commanding Officer. CAPT Willard H. Brownson. Rated as COAST BATTLESHIP NO. 8. Placed in comm., in reserve, 3 Nov 1908 at Brooklyn, NY. Decomm. 17 Aug 1909 at Brooklyn, NY. Placed in comm., in reserve, 1 Jul 1912. Placed in full comm. 25 Jul 1912. Placed in comm., in reserve, 10 Sep 1912 at Brooklyn, NY. Placed in ordinary 31 Oct 1913. Placed in comm., in reserve, 1 Jul 1914 at Philadelphia, PA. Recomm. 5 Apr 1917. Decomm. 7 May 1920 at Norfolk, VA. Classified BB-8 on 17 Jul 1920. Struck 15 Sep 1921 from the NVR. Trans. 15 Sep 1921 to the War Department. Sunk 27 Sep 1921 as a bombing target by the Army Air Corps in Chesapeake Bay. Raised and sold 19 Mar 1924 to the Union Shipbuilding Co., Baltimore, MD. Scrapped.

Alabama BB-8 — Photograph taken, early 1900s, anchored in an unknown harbor. (Ray D. Bean photo collection)

Alabama BB-8 — Photograph taken, 12 October 1912, anchored at New York City, NY, during a naval review. (Ray D. Bean photo collection)

Wisconsin (BB-9)

NAME (HULL NO.)	BUILDER	KEEL LAID	LAUNCHED	COMMISSIONED
WISCONSIN (BB-9)	Union Iron	9 Feb 1897	26 Nov 1898	4 Feb 1901

Authorized 10 Jun 1896. Contract awarded 19 Sep 1896. Sponsored by Miss Elizabeth Stephenson. First Commanding Officer: CAPT George C. Reiter. Rated as COAST BATTLESHIP NO. 9. Decomm. 15 Nov 1906 at Bremerton, WA. Recomm. 1 Apr 1908. Placed in comm., in reserve, 27 Apr 1910 at Portsmouth, NH. Placed in ordinary 31 Oct 1913. Placed in full comm. 15 Apr 1915. Placed in comm., in reserve, 15 Oct 1915 at Philadelphia, PA. Placed in full comm. 2 May 1916. Placed in comm., in reserve, 1916 at Philadelphia, PA. Recomm. 24 Apr 1917. Decomm. 15 May 1920 at Philadelphia, PA. Classified BB-9 on 17 Jul 1920. Struck from the NVR. Sold 26 Jan 1922. Scrapped.

Wisconsin BB-9 — Photograph taken, early 1903, anchored in Puget Sound, WA. Note the civilians standing around the bow. (Ray D. Bean photo collection)

Wisconsin BB-9 — Photograph taken, 12 October 1912, anchored at New York City, NY, during a naval review.

Class Specifications			As Completed (1900/1901)	Operational Condition as of 1919
HULL	LENGTH	Waterline	368’ 0”	368’ 0”
		Overall	375’ 4” (BB-7)	375’ 4” (BB-7)
			374’ 0” (BB-8)	374’ 0” (BB-8)
			373’ 10” (BB-9)	373’ 10” (BB-9)
	EXTREME BEAM		72’ 3”	72’ 2.5”
	DISPLACEMENT	Full Load	12,170 tons (BB-7, 8)	12,100 tons
			12,571 tons (BB-9)	
		Normal	11,565 tons	11,552 tons
	MAXIMUM DRAFT		26’ 1” (BB-7)	24’ 9”
			26’ 0” (BB-8)	
			25’ 9” (BB-9)	
	COMPLEMENT	Officers	40 (BB-7, 8)	52
			34 (BB-9)	
		Enlisted	496 (BB-7, 8)	765
			556 (BB-9)	
ARMAMENT		Main	(2) twin 13”/35 B.L.R. turrets	(2) twin 13”/35 B.L.R. turrets
		Secondary	(14) single 6”/40 R.F. mounts	(8) single 6”/40 R.F. mounts
			(16) single 6 pdr.	(2) single 3”/50 mounts
			(7) single 1 pdr. (BB-7, 9)	(4) single 6 pdr. saluting (BB-9)
			(8) single 1 pdr. (BB-8)	(2) single 6 pdr. saluting (BB-7, 8)
			(4) colt mg.	
		Torpedo Tubes	(4) 18” surface	None
	ARMOR	Belt		
		Top	16.5”	16.5”
		Bottom	9.5”	9.5”
		Waterline	13.75”	13.1” – 13.2.5”
		Bulkheads	12”	12”
		Deck		
		Forward	2.75” – 3”	2.75” – 3”
		Aft	2.75” – 5”	2.75” – 4”
		Amidships	2.75”	2.75”
		Turrets	14”	14”
		Barbettes	10” – 15”	10”– 15”
		Conning Tower	10”	10”
ENGINEERING	SPEED	Maximum	17.5 knots (BB-7)	17.5 knots (BB-7)
			17.0 knots (BB-8)	17.0 knots (BB-8)
			17.2 knots (BB-9)	17.2 knots (BB-9)
		Economical	10.0 knots	10.0 knots
	ENGINES	Manufacturer	Newport News (BB-7)	Newport News (BB-7)
			Cramp (BB-8)	Cramp (BB-8)
			Union (BB-9)	Union (BB-9)
		Type	Vert. 3-Exp. Recip.	Vert. 3-Exp. Recip.
	HORSEPOWER	Indicated	12,899 (BB-7)	12,899 (BB-7)
			11,366 (BB-8)	11,366 (BB-8)
			12,609 (BB-9)	12,609 (BB 9)
	SCREWS		2	2
	BOILERS	Manufacturer	Newport News (BB-7)	Mosher (BB-7)
			Cramp (BB-8)	Cramp (BB-8)
			Union (BB-9)	Union (BB-9)
		Type/No.	FT (Scotch)/8	WT/8 (BB-7)
				Single-ended cylindrical
				FT (Scotch)/8 (BB-8, 9)
	FUEL CAPACITY		1,400 tons coal (BB-7)	1,522 tons coal (BB-7)
			1,355 tons coal (BB-8)	1,481 tons coal (BB-8)
			1,310 tons coal (BB-9)	1,447 tons coal (BB-9)

7: MAINE CLASS (BB-10 to BB-12)

Maine (BB-10)

NAME (HULL NO.)	BUILDER	KEEL LAID	LAUNCHED	COMMISSIONED
MAINE (BB-10)	W. Cramp	15 Feb 1899	27 Jul 1901	29 Dec 1902

Authorized 4 May 1898. Contract awarded 1 Oct 1898. Sponsored by Miss Mary P. Anderson. First Commanding Officer: CAPT Eugene H. C. Leutze. Rated as COAST BATTLESHIP NO. 10. Decomm. 31 Aug 1909 at Portsmouth, NH. Recomm. 15 Jun 1911. Placed in comm., in reserve, 6 Dec 1911 at Philadelphia, PA. Placed in full comm. 4 Jul 1914. Placed in comm., in reserve, 18 Sep 1914 at Brooklyn, NY. Decomm. 31 Oct 1919 at Philadelphia, PA. Classified BB-10 on 17 Jul 1920. Struck from the NVR. Sold 26 Jan 1922 to Mr. Joseph G. Hitner & Mr. William F. Cutler, Philadelphia, Pa. Demilitarization completed by 17 Dec 1923 in accordance with the terms of the Washington Treaty for Naval Limitations. Scrapped.

Maine BB-10 — Photograph taken, early 1909, anchored in an unknown harbor. Note that the boat booms extended from the port and starboard sides of the ship. (Ray D. Bean photo collection)

Maine BB-10 — Photograph taken, between 1911 and 1916, while underway at high speed along the East Coast of the United States.

Missouri (BB-11)

NAME (HULL NO.)	BUILDER	KEEL LAID	LAUNCHED	COMMISSIONED
MISSOURI (BB-11)	NNS&DD Co.	7 Feb 1900	28 Dec 1901	1 Dec 1903

Authorized 4 May 1898. Contract awarded 30 Dec 1898. Sponsored by Miss Marion Cockrell. First Commanding Officer: CAPT William S. Cowles. Rated as COAST BATTLESHIP NO. 11. Placed in comm., in reserve, 2 May 1910 at Boston, MA. Placed in full comm. 1 Jun 1911. Decomm. 16 Oct 1912 at Philadelphia, PA. Recomm. 16 Mar 1914. Placed in ordinary 2 Dec 1914 at Philadelphia, PA. Placed in full comm. 15 Apr 1915. Placed in comm., in reserve, 15 Oct 1915 at Philadelphia, PA. Placed in full comm. 2 May 1916. Placed in ordinary at Philadelphia, PA. Recomm. 23 Apr 1917. Decomm. 8 Sep 1919 at Philadelphia, PA. Classified BB-11 on 17 Jul 1920. Struck from the NVR. Sold 26 Jan 1922 to Mr. Joseph G. Hitner & Mr. William F. Cutler, Philadelphia, PA. Demilitarization completed by 17 Dec 1923 in accordance with the terms of the Washington Treaty for Naval Limitations. Scrapped.

Missouri BB-11 — Photograph taken, circa 1902, while underway at high speed on sea trials shortly before commissioning. (Official U.S. Navy Photo)

Missouri BB-11 — Photograph taken, circa 1909, anchored at an unknown location along the East Coast of the United States. (U.S. Naval History and Heritage Command Photo)

Missouri BB-11 — Photograph taken, 1912, anchored at New York City, NY, during a naval review. (U.S. Naval History and Heritage Command Photo)

Ohio (BB-12)

NAME (HULL NO.)	BUILDER	KEEL LAID	LAUNCHED	COMMISSIONED
OHIO (BB-12)	Union Iron	22 Apr 1899	18 May 1901	4 Oct 1904

Authorized 4 May 1898. Contract awarded 5 Oct 1898. Sponsored by Miss Helen Deshler. First Commanding Officer: CAPT Leavitt C. Logan. Rated as COAST BATTLESHIP NO. 12. Decomm. 20 Dec 1909 at Brooklyn, NY. Recomm. 1 Jun 1911. Placed in comm., in reserve, 18 Apr 1914 at Philadelphia, PA. Placed in full comm. 15 Apr 1915. Placed in comm., in reserve, 15 Oct 1915 at Philadelphia, PA. Placed in full comm. 2 May 1916. Recomm. 24 Apr 1917. Placed in comm., in reserve, 7 Jan 1919 at Philadelphia, PA. Classified BB-12 on 17 Jul 1920. Decomm. 31 May 1922 at Philadelphia, PA. Demilitarized in accordance with the terms of the Washington Treaty for Naval Limitations. Sold 24 Mar 1923. Scrapped.

Ohio BB-12 — Photograph taken, July 1904, anchored in San Francisco Bay, CA, after completion of builder's sea trials. (U.S. Naval History and Heritage Command Photo)

Ohio BB-12 — Photograph taken, 16 July 1915, while underway being towed passing Cucaracha Slide going through the Panama Canal. (Ray D. Bean photo collection)

Ohio BB-12 — Photograph taken, 10 October 1920, anchored in an unknown harbor on the East Coast of the United States. Note the boat booms extended from the port and starboard sides of the ship.

Class Specifications			As Completed (1902/1904)	Operational Condition as of 1919
HULL	LENGTH	Waterline	388' 0"	388' 0"
		Overall	393' 11" (BB-10, 11)	393' 11" (BB-10, 11)
			393' 10" (BB-12)	393' 10" (BB-12)
	EXTREME BEAM		72' 3"	72' 2.5"
	DISPLACEMENT	Full Load	13,500 tons	13,500 tons
		Normal	12,500 tons	12,500 tons
	MAXIMUM DRAFT		25' 6" (BB-10)	25' 6" (BB-10)
			25' 7" (BB-11)	25' 8" (BB-11)
			25' 10" (BB-12)	25' 4" (BB-12)
	COMPLEMENT	Officers	34 (BB-10)	53 (BB-10)
			40 (BB-11)	52 (BB-11)
			41 (BB-12)	55 (BB-12)
		Enlisted	612 (BB-10), 521 (BB-11)	964 (BB-10, 11)
			663 (BB-12)	992 (BB-12)
		Marines	None	5
ARMAMENT		Main	(2) twin 12"/40 B.L.R. turrets	(2) twin 12"/40 B.L.R. turrets
		Secondary	(16) single 6"/50 R.F. mounts	(8) single 6"/50 R.F. mounts
			(6) single 3"/50 R.F. mounts	(2) single 3"/50 R.F. mounts
			(8) single 3 pdr.	(2) single 6 pdr. saluting (BB-12)
			(6) single 1 pdr. (BB-10, 12)	(4) single 3 pdr. saluting (BB-10)
			(4) single 1 pdr. (BB-11)	(2) single 3 pdr. saluting (BB-11)
			(2) colt mg.	
		Torpedo Tubes	(2) 18" submerged	(2) 18" submerged
	ARMOR	Belt		
		Top	11"	11"
		Bottom	7.5"	7.5"
		Waterline	11"	11"
		Bulkheads	9"	9"
		Deck		
		Forward	2.5" – 2.75" (BB-10, 12)	2.5" – 2.75" (BB-10, 12)
			2.5" – 3" (BB-11)	2.5" – 3" (BB-11)
		Aft	2.75" – 4" (BB-10, 12)	2.75" – 4" (BB-10, 12)
			2.5" – 4" (BB-11)	2.5" – 4" (BB-11)
		Amidships	2.5"	2.5"
		Turrets	11" – 12"	11" – 12"
		Barbettes	8" – 12"	8" – 12"
		Conning Tower	10"	10"
ENGINEERING	SPEED	Maximum	18.3 knots (BB-10)	18.0 knots (BB-10)
			18.2 knots (BB-11)	18.2 knots (BB-11)
			17.8 knots (BB-12)	17.8 knots (BB-12)
		Economical	10.0 knots	10.0 knots
	ENGINES	Manufacturer	Cramp (BB-10)	Cramp (BB-10)
			Newport News (BB-11)	Newport News (BB-11)
			Union (BB-12)	Union (BB-12)
		Type	Vert. 3-Exp. Recip.	Vert. 3-Exp. Recip.
	HORSEPOWER	Indicated	15,603 (BB-10)	15,841 (BB-10)
			15,845 (BB-11)	16,277 (BB-11)
			16,220 (BB-12)	16,507 (BB-12)
	SCREWS		2	2
	BOILERS	Manufacturer	Niclausse (BB-10)	B & W (BB-10)
			Newport News (BB-11)	Newport News (BB-11)
			Union (BB-12)	Union (BB-12)
		Type/No.	WT/12 (BB-10)	WT/12 (BB-10)
			Thornycroft WT/12 (BB-11, 12)	Thornycroft WT/12 (BB-11, 12)
	FUEL CAPACITY		1,875 tons coal (BB-10)	1,904 tons coal (BB-10)
			1,825 tons coal (BB-11)	1,933 tons coal (BB-11)
			2,150 tons coal (BB-12)	2,331 tons coal (BB-12)

8: VIRGINIA CLASS (BB-13 to BB-17)

Virginia (BB-13)

NAME (HULL NO.)	BUILDER	KEEL LAID	LAUNCHED	COMMISSIONED
VIRGINIA (BB-13)	NNS&DD Co.	21 May 1902	5 Apr 1904	7 May 1906

Authorized 3 Mar 1899. Contract awarded 15 Feb 1901. Sponsored by Miss Mathilde G. Montague. First Commanding Officer: CAPT Seaton Schroeder. Rated as COAST BATTLESHIP NO. 13. Placed in comm., in reserve, 20 Mar 1916 at Boston, MA. Recomm. 6 Apr 1917. Classified BB-13 on 17 Jul 1920. Decomm. 13 Aug 1920 at Boston, MA. Struck 12 Jul 1922 from the NVR. Trans. 6 Aug 1923 to the War Department. Sunk 5 Sep 1923 as a bombing target by the Army Air Corps off Cape Hatteras, NC.

Virginia BB-13 — Photograph taken, circa 1906–1907, tied up to a pier at an unknown location on the East Coast of the United States. (U.S. Naval History and Heritage Command Photo)

Virginia BB-13 — Photograph taken, circa 1914–1916, while underway in Hampton Roads, VA. Note that her crew are manning the rails in their whites. (U.S. Naval History and Heritage Command Photo)

Virginia BB-13 — Photograph taken, circa 1918, anchored after receiving World War I alterations at an unknown location along the East Coast of the United States. Note that her aft six-inch broadside guns had been removed. This was done in order to provide additional berthing for troops coming back after the war. (U.S. Naval History and Heritage Command Photo)

Nebraska (BB-14)

NAME (HULL NO.)	BUILDER	KEEL LAID	LAUNCHED	COMMISSIONED
NEBRASKA (BB-14)	Moran Bros.	4 Jul 1902	7 Oct 1904	1 Jul 1907

Authorized 3 Mar 1899. Contract awarded 7 Mar 1901. Sponsored by Miss Mary N. Mickey. First Commanding Officer: CAPT Reginald F. Nicholson. Rated as COAST BATTLESHIP NO. 14. Originally named PENNSYLVANIA. Renamed NEBRASKA 1901. Placed in comm., in reserve, 15 May 1916 at Boston, MA. Placed in full comm. 3 Apr 1917. Decomm. 2 Jul 1920. Classified BB-14 on 17 Jul 1920. Struck 12 Jul 1922 from the NVR. Demilitarization completed by 9 Nov 1923 in accordance with the terms of the Washington Treaty for Naval Limitations. Sold 30 Nov 1923. Scrapped.

Nebraska BB-14 — Photograph taken, 1908, anchored in a West Coast harbor. Note the ship's name in large letters mounted on the front of the bridge. (U.S. Naval History and Heritage Command Photo)

Nebraska BB-14 — Photograph taken, 3 October 1911, anchored in the Hudson River, off of New York City, NY. Note the crew's laundry hanging on lines from the bridge to the bow and the Palisade Amusement Park in the distance off to the right. (U.S. Naval History and Heritage Command Photo)

Nebraska BB-14 — Photograph taken, 1918, while underway at an unknown location along the East Coast of the United States. Note that she was painted in a "Watson/Norfolk" Scheme 3 experimental camouflage pattern. (U.S. Naval History and Heritage Command Photo)

Georgia (BB-15)

NAME (HULL NO.)	BUILDER	KEEL LAID	LAUNCHED	COMMISSIONED
GEORGIA (BB-15)	Bath Iron	31 Aug 1901	11 Oct 1904	24 Sep 1906

Authorized 3 Mar 1899. Contract awarded 18 Feb 1901. Sponsored by Miss Stella Tate. First Commanding Officer: CAPT Richard G. Davenport. Rated as COAST BATTLESHIP NO. 15. Placed in comm., in reserve, 3 Feb 1916 at Boston, MA. Recomm. 6 Apr 1917. Decomm. 15 Jul 1920 at Vallejo, CA. Classified BB-15 on 17 Jul 1920. Struck 12 Jul 1922 from the NVR. Demilitarization completed by 4 Oct 1923 in accordance with the terms of the Washington Treaty for Naval Limitations. Sold 1 Nov 1923 to Mr. Louis Rothenberg, Oakland, CA. Scrapped.

Georgia BB-15 — Photograph taken, 11 October 1904, during her launching at Bath, ME. Note that the submerged torpedo tube was plated over just above and a little aft of the forward launch cradle. (Ray D. Bean photo collection)

Georgia BB-15 — Photograph taken, between September--December 1918, at Newport News, VA. Note that most of her secondary armament had been removed. This was done in order to provide additional berthing for troops coming back after the war.

New Jersey (BB-16)

NAME (HULL NO.)	BUILDER	KEEL LAID	LAUNCHED	COMMISSIONED
NEW JERSEY (BB-16)	Fore R S & E	2 Apr 1902	10 Nov 1904	12 May 1906

Authorized 7 Jun 1900. Contract awarded 15 Feb 1901. Sponsored by Mrs. William B. Kinny. First Commanding Officer: CAPT William W. Kimball. Rated as COAST BATTLESHIP NO. 16. Placed in comm., in reserve, 2 May 1910 at Boston, MA. Placed in full comm. 15 Jul 1911. Placed in comm., in reserve, 15 May 1916 at Boston, MA. Classified BB-16 on 17 Jul 1920. Decomm. 6 Aug 1920 at Boston, MA. Struck 12 Jul 1922 from the NVR. Trans. to the War Department. Sunk 5 Sep 1923 as a bombing target by the Army Air Corps off Cape Hatteras, NC.

New Jersey BB-16 — Photograph taken, late August 1908, anchored in Sydney Harbor, Australia, as part of the "Great White Fleet." (Official U.S. Navy Photo)

New Jersey BB-16 — Photograph taken, circa 1918, anchored at an unknown location along the East Coast of the United States. Note that the ship was painted in a MacKay "disruptive low-visibility pattern" and being used for testing against naval shipboard range finders. (Official U.S. Navy Photo)

Rhode Island (BB-17)

NAME (HULL NO.)	BUILDER	KEEL LAID	LAUNCHED	COMMISSIONED
RHODE ISLAND (BB-17)	Fore R S & E	1 May 1902	17 May 1904	19 Feb 1906

Authorized 7 Jun 1900. Contract awarded 15 Feb 1901. Sponsored by Mrs. Frederic C. Dumaine. First Commanding Officer: CAPT Perry Garst. Rated as COAST BATTLESHIP NO. 17. Decomm. 30 Jun 1920 at Vallejo, CA. Classified BB-17 on 17 Jun 1920. Struck 12 Jul 1922 from the NVR. Demilitarization completed by 4 Oct 1923 in accordance with the terms of the Washington Treaty for Naval Limitations. Sold 1 Nov 1923. Scrapped.

Rhode Island BB-17 — Photograph taken, 8 July 1909, while underway leaving the New York Navy Yard, Brooklyn, NY. Note that she had been refitted with a "cage" foremast, but still retained her military mainmast aft.

Rhode Island BB-17 — Photograph taken, circa 1906, just before commissioning while still in the builders yard. (Ray D. Bean photo collection)

Rhode Island BB-17 — Photograph taken, 17 July 1913, anchored in New York City, NY. (Ray D. Bean photo collection)

<table>
<tr><th colspan="3">Class Specifications</th><th>As Completed (1906/1907)</th><th>Operational Condition as of 1919</th></tr>
<tr><td rowspan="13">HULL</td><td rowspan="2">LENGTH</td><td>Waterline</td><td>435’ 0”</td><td>435’ 0”</td></tr>
<tr><td>Overall</td><td>441’ 3”</td><td>441’ 3”</td></tr>
<tr><td colspan="2">EXTREME BEAM</td><td>76’ 2.5”</td><td>76’ 2.5”</td></tr>
<tr><td rowspan="2">DISPLACEMENT</td><td>Full Load</td><td>16,094 tons</td><td>16,094 tons</td></tr>
<tr><td>Normal</td><td>14,948 tons</td><td>14,948 tons</td></tr>
<tr><td colspan="2">MAXIMUM DRAFT</td><td>26’ 0”</td><td>25’ 10”</td></tr>
<tr><td rowspan="7">COMPLEMENT</td><td rowspan="2">Officers</td><td rowspan="2">40</td><td>66 (BB-15)</td></tr>
<tr><td>63 (BB-13, 14, 16, 17)</td></tr>
<tr><td rowspan="4">Enlisted</td><td rowspan="4">772</td><td>1,067 (BB-16)</td></tr>
<tr><td>1,041 (BB-13)</td></tr>
<tr><td>1,040 (BB-15)</td></tr>
<tr><td>1,012 (BB-14, 17)</td></tr>
<tr><td>Marines</td><td>None</td><td>5 (BB-13, 15)</td></tr>
<tr><td rowspan="26">ARMAMENT</td><td rowspan="8"></td><td rowspan="2">Main</td><td>(2) twin 12”/40 B.L.R. turrets</td><td>(2) twin 12”/40 B.L.R. turrets</td></tr>
<tr><td>(4) twin 8”/45 B.L.R. turrets</td><td>(4) twin 8”/45 B.L.R. turrets</td></tr>
<tr><td rowspan="5">Secondary</td><td>(12) single 6”/50 mounts</td><td>(8) single 3”/50 R.F. mounts (BB-13 to 16)</td></tr>
<tr><td>(12) single 3”/50 R.F. mounts</td><td>(2) single 3”/50 A.A. mounts</td></tr>
<tr><td>(12) single 3 pdr.</td><td>(2) single 6 pdr. saluting (BB-15)</td></tr>
<tr><td>(2) single 1 pdr.</td><td>(4) single 3 pdr. saluting (BB-16)</td></tr>
<tr><td>(2) colt mg.</td><td>(2) single 3 pdr. saluting (BB-14)</td></tr>
<tr><td>Torpedo Tubes</td><td>(4) 21” submerged</td><td>(4) 21” submerged</td></tr>
<tr><td rowspan="18">ARMOR</td><td colspan="3">Belt</td></tr>
<tr><td>Top</td><td>11”</td><td>11”</td></tr>
<tr><td>Bottom</td><td>8”</td><td>8”</td></tr>
<tr><td>Waterline</td><td>11”</td><td>11”</td></tr>
<tr><td colspan="3">Deck</td></tr>
<tr><td>Forward</td><td>3”</td><td>3”</td></tr>
<tr><td>Aft</td><td>3”</td><td>3”</td></tr>
<tr><td>Amidships</td><td>1.5” – 3”</td><td>1.5” – 3”</td></tr>
<tr><td rowspan="2">12” Gun Turrets</td><td rowspan="2">6” – 12”</td><td>6” – 12.8” (BB-13, 15 to 17)</td></tr>
<tr><td>6” – 12” (BB-14)</td></tr>
<tr><td>8” Gun Turrets</td><td>6” – 6.5”</td><td>6” – 6.5”</td></tr>
<tr><td>12” Gun Barbettes</td><td>7.5” – 10”</td><td>7.5” – 10”</td></tr>
<tr><td rowspan="3">8” Gun Barbettes</td><td rowspan="3">4” – 6”</td><td>6” – 6.5” (BB-13)</td></tr>
<tr><td>4” – 6” (BB-15 to 17)</td></tr>
<tr><td>6” (BB-14)</td></tr>
<tr><td>Conning Tower</td><td>9”</td><td>9”</td></tr>
<tr><td rowspan="24">ENGINEERING</td><td rowspan="5">SPEED</td><td rowspan="4">Maximum</td><td>19.0 knots (BB-13, 17)</td><td>19.0 knots (BB-13, 17)</td></tr>
<tr><td>19.1 knots (BB-14)</td><td>19.1 knots (BB-14)</td></tr>
<tr><td>19.3 knots (BB-15)</td><td>19.3 knots (BB-15)</td></tr>
<tr><td>19.2 knots (BB-16)</td><td>19.2 knots (BB-16)</td></tr>
<tr><td>Economical</td><td>10.0 knots</td><td>10.0 knots</td></tr>
<tr><td rowspan="5">ENGINES</td><td rowspan="4">Manufacturer</td><td>Newport News (BB-13)</td><td>Newport News (BB-13)</td></tr>
<tr><td>Moran (BB-14)</td><td>Moran (BB-14)</td></tr>
<tr><td>Bath (BB-15)</td><td>Bath (BB-15)</td></tr>
<tr><td>Fore R S & E (BB-16, 17)</td><td>Fore R S & E (BB-16, 17)</td></tr>
<tr><td>Type</td><td>Vert. 3-Exp. Recip.</td><td>Vert. 3-Exp. Recip.</td></tr>
<tr><td rowspan="5">HORSEPOWER</td><td rowspan="5">Indicated</td><td>22,841 (BB-13)</td><td>23,468 (BB-13)</td></tr>
<tr><td>21,283 (BB-14)</td><td>21,911 (BB-14)</td></tr>
<tr><td>25,088 (BB-15)</td><td>25,643 (BB-15)</td></tr>
<tr><td>23,089 (BB-16)</td><td>23,570 (BB-16)</td></tr>
<tr><td>20,310 (BB-17)</td><td>20,627 (BB-17)</td></tr>
<tr><td colspan="2">SCREWS</td><td>2</td><td>2</td></tr>
<tr><td rowspan="4">BOILERS</td><td rowspan="2">Manufacturer</td><td>Niclausse (BB-13, 15)</td><td>B & W</td></tr>
<tr><td>B & W (BB-14, 16, 17)</td><td></td></tr>
<tr><td rowspan="2">Type/No.</td><td>WT/24 (BB-13, 15)</td><td>WT/12</td></tr>
<tr><td>WT/12 (BB-14, 16, 17)</td><td></td></tr>
<tr><td colspan="2" rowspan="4">FUEL CAPACITY</td><td>1,900 tons coal (BB-13)</td><td>1,970 tons coal (BB-13)</td></tr>
<tr><td>1,775 tons coal (BB-14)</td><td>1,969 tons coal (BB-14)</td></tr>
<tr><td>1,925 tons coal (BB-15)</td><td>2,014 tons coal (BB-15)</td></tr>
<tr><td>2,000 tons coal (BB-16, 17)</td><td>1,993 tons coal (BB-16)</td></tr>
</table>

Connecticut (BB-18)

NAME (HULL NO.)	BUILDER	KEEL LAID	LAUNCHED	COMMISSIONED
CONNECTICUT (BB-18)	New York NY	10 Mar 1903	29 Sep 1904	29 Sep 1906

Authorized 1 Jul 1902. Contract awarded 15 Oct 1902. Sponsored by Miss Alice Wells. First Commanding Officer: CAPT William Swift. Rated as BATTLESHIP NO. 18. Placed in comm., in reserve, 12 May 1915 at Philadelphia, PA. Placed in full comm. 3 Oct 1916. Classified BB-18 on 17 Jul 1920. Decomm. 1 Mar 1923 at Bremerton, WA. Demilitarization completed by 12 Oct 1923 in accordance with the terms of the Washington Treaty for Naval Limitations. Struck 10 Nov 1923 from the NVR. Sold 1 Nov 1923 to Mr. Walter W. Johnson, San Francisco, CA, for $42,750.00. Scrapped.

Connecticut BB-18 — Photograph taken, 29 March 1905, while being fitted out at the New York Navy Yard, Brooklyn, NY. Note the armor plates being lifted in place against the teak wood backing of the ship.

Connecticut BB-18 — Photograph taken, 1910, while underway in a unknown harbor along the East Coast of the United States. Note that the crew were at their sea and anchor detail stations. (Official U.S. Navy Photo)

Connecticut BB-18 — Photograph taken, 2 November 1911, anchored in the Hudson River, New York City, NY. Note that the ship was firing a gun salute to President William H. Taft. (Ray D. Bean photo collection)

Connecticut BB-18 — Photograph taken, circa 1923–1924, tied up to a pier at a shipyard in Oakland, CA, being scrapped. (U.S. Naval History and Heritage Command Photo)

NAME (HULL NO.)	BUILDER	KEEL LAID	LAUNCHED	COMMISSIONED
LOUISIANA (BB-19)	NNS&DD Co.	7 Feb 1903	27 Aug 1904	2 Jun 1906

Authorized 1 Jul 1902. Contract awarded 15 Oct 1902. Sponsored by Miss Juanita La Lande. First Commanding Officer: CAPT Albert R. Couden. Rated as BATTLESHIP NO. 19. Placed in comm., in reserve, 16 May 1916 at Portsmouth, VA. Classified BB-19 on 17 Jul 1920. Decomm. 20 Oct 1920 at Philadelphia, PA. Demilitarization completed by 25 Sep 1923 in accordance with the terms of the Washington Treaty for Naval Limitations. Struck 10 Nov 1923 from the NVR. Sold 1 Nov 1923. Scrapped.

Louisiana BB-19 — Photograph taken, 17 May 1906, tied up to a pier at the Newport News Shipbuilding & Dry Dock Co., Newport News, VA, two weeks before her commissioning.

Louisiana BB-19 — Photograph taken, 2 November 1911, anchored in the Hudson River, New York City, NY. Note that the ship was firing a gun salute to President William H. Taft. (Ray D. Bean photo collection)

Vermont (BB-20)

NAME (HULL NO.)	BUILDER	KEEL LAID	LAUNCHED	COMMISSIONED
VERMONT (BB-20)	Fore R S & E	21 May 1904	31 Aug 1905	4 Mar 1907

Authorized 3 Mar 1903. Contract awarded 20 Jun 1903. Sponsored by Miss Jennie Bell. First Commanding Officer: CAPT William P. Potter. Rated as BATTLESHIP NO. 20. Placed in comm., in reserve, 1 Oct 1916 at Philadelphia, PA. Placed in full comm. 21 Nov 1916. Decomm. 30 Jun 1920 at Vallejo, CA. Classified BB-20 on 17 Jul 1920. Demilitarization completed by 9 Nov 1923 in accordance with the terms of the Washington Treaty for Naval Limitations. Struck 10 Nov 1923 from the NVR. Sold 30 Nov 1923. Scrapped.

Vermont BB-20 — Photograph taken, 20 August 1907, anchored in Hampton Roads, VA.

Vermont BB-20 — Photograph taken, late August 1908, anchored in Sydney Harbor, Australia, as part of the "Great White Fleet." (Official U.S. Navy Photo)

Vermont BB-20 — Photograph taken, 8 June 1913, anchored in Chesapeake Bay, MD, after embarking midshipmen from the U.S. Naval Academy for a summer training cruise. Note her military masts had been replaced with "cage" masts.

NAME (HULL NO.)	BUILDER	KEEL LAID	LAUNCHED	COMMISSIONED
KANSAS (BB-21)	NY Ship Co.	10 Feb 1904	12 Aug 1905	18 Apr 1907

Authorized 3 Mar 1903. Contract awarded 16 Jun 1903. Sponsored by Miss Anna Hoch. First Commanding Officer: CAPT Charles E. Vreeland. Rated as BATTLESHIP NO. 21. Classified BB-21 on 17 Jul 1920. Decomm. 16 Dec 1921 at Philadelphia, PA. Demilitarization completed by 9 Oct 1923 in accordance with the terms of the Washington Treaty for Naval Limitations. Struck 10 Nov 1923 from the NVR. Sold 23 Jan 1924. Scrapped.

Kansas BB-21 — Photograph taken, late August 1908, anchored in Sydney Harbor, Australia, as part of the "Great White Fleet." (Official U.S. Navy Photo)

Kansas BB-21 — Photograph taken, 23 June 1912, anchored at Annapolis, MD, where she embarked midshipmen from the U.S. Naval Academy for a summer training cruise.

Minnesota (BB-22)

NAME (HULL NO.)	BUILDER	KEEL LAID	LAUNCHED	COMMISSIONED
MINNESOTA (BB-22)	NNS&DD Co.	27 Oct 1903	8 Apr 1905	9 Mar 1907

Authorized 3 Mar 1903. Contract awarded 20 Jun 1903. Sponsored by Miss Rose M. Schaller. First Commanding Officer: CAPT John Hubbard. Rated as BATTLESHIP NO. 22. Decomm. November 1916. Recomm. 6 Apr 1917. Classified BB-22 on 17 Jul 1920. Decomm. 1 Dec 1921 at Philadelphia, PA. Demilitarization completed by 9 Oct 1923 in accordance with the terms of the Washington Treaty for Naval Limitations. Struck 10 Nov 1923 from the NVR. Sold 23 Jan 1924. Scrapped.

Minnesota BB-22 — Photograph taken, 1906, while underway at high speed, making 18.18 knots during builder's sea trials at an unknown location along the East Coast of the United States.

New Hampshire (BB-25)

NAME (HULL NO.)	BUILDER	KEEL LAID	LAUNCHED	COMMISSIONED
NEW HAMPSHIRE (BB-25)	NY Ship Co.	1 May 1905	30 Jun 1906	19 Mar 1908

Authorized 27 Apr 1904. Contract awarded 27 Apr 1904. Sponsored by Miss Hazel E. McLane. First Commanding Officer: CAPT Cameron M. Winslow. Rated as BATTLESHIP NO. 25. Classified BB-25 on 17 Jul 1920. Decomm. 21 May 1921 at Philadelphia, PA. Demilitarization completed by 18 Sep 1923 in accordance with the terms of the Washington Treaty for Naval Limitations. Struck 10 Nov 1923 from the NVR. Sold 1 Nov 1923. Scrapped.

New Hampshire BB-25 — Photograph taken, 19 December 1907, while underway at high speed, making 18.30 knots during builder's sea trials off Rockland, ME. Note that her turrets had not yet been installed.

New Hampshire BB-25 — Photograph taken, circa 1910, anchored in a unknown harbor along the East Coast of the United States. (Ray D. Bean photo collection)

Class Specifications			As Completed (1906/1908)	Operational Condition as of 1919
HULL	LENGTH	Waterline	450' 0"	450' 0"
		Overall	456' 4"	456' 4" BB-18, 19, 21, 22, 25)
				455' 10" (BB-20)
	EXTREME BEAM		76' 10"	76' 10"
	DISPLACEMENT	Full Load	17,666 tons (BB-18, 19)	17,666 tons (BB-18, 19)
			17,650 tons (BB-20 to 22)	17,650 tons (BB-20 to 22)
			17,784 tons (BB-25)	17,784 tons (BB-25)
		Normal	16,000 tons	16,000 tons
	MAXIMUM DRAFT		26' 8" (BB-18 to 22)	26' 8" (BB-18, 19, 21, 22)
			27' 0" (BB-25)	25' 10" (BB-20)
				27' 0" (BB-25)
	COMPLEMENT	Officers	41	66 (BB-18, 19, 22)
				63 (BB-20, 21, 25)
		Enlisted	855 (BB-18)	1,171 (BB-18)
			840 (BB-19, 20, 22)	1,172 (BB-19)
			809 (BB-21, 25)	1,143 (BB-20 to 22, 25)
		Marines	None	5 (BB-18, 19)
ARMAMENT		Main	(2) twin 12"/45 B.L.R. turrets	(2) twin 12"/45 B.L.R. turrets
			(4) twin 8"/45 B.L.R. turrets	(4) twin 8"/45 B.L.R. turrets
		Secondary	(12) single 7"/45 B.L.R. mounts	(12) single 3"/50 R.F. mounts
			(20) single 3"/50 R.F. mounts	(2) single 3"/50 A.A. mounts
			(4) single 6 pdr. (BB-19 to 22, 25)	(4) single 6 pdr. saluting (BB-22)
			(4) single 3 pdr. (BB-18, 25)	(2) single 6 pdr. saluting (BB-19, 21, 25)
			(4) single 1 pdr. (BB-18, 20)	
			(2) single 1 pdr. (BB-19, 21, 22, 25)	
		Torpedo Tubes	(4) 21" submerged	(4) 21" submerged
	ARMOR	Belt		
		Top	11" (BB-18, 19)	11" (BB-18, 19)
			9" (BB-20 to 22, 25)	9" (BB-20 to 22, 25)
		Bottom	9"	9"
		Waterline	11" (BB-18, 19)	11" (BB-18, 19)
			9" (BB-20 to 22, 25)	9" (BB-20 to 22, 25)
		Bulkheads	6"	6"
		Deck		
		Forward	3"	3"
		Aft	3"	3"
		Amidships	1.5" – 3"	1.5" – 3"

ARMAMENT	ARMOR	12" Gun Turrets	8" – 12"	8" – 12"
		8" Gun Turrets	6" – 6.5"	6" – 6.5"
		12" Gun Barbettes	7.5" – 10" (BB-18 to 22)	7.5" – 10" (BB-18 to 22)
			7.5" – 11" (BB-25)	7.5" – 11" (BB-25)
		8" Gun Barbettes	4" – 6" (BB-18, 19, 21, 22, 25)	4" – 6" (BB-18, 19, 21, 22, 25)
			6" (BB-20)	6" (BB-20)
		Conning Tower	9"	9"
ENGINEERING	SPEED	Maximum	18.8 knots (BB-18, 19)	18.8 knots (BB-18, 19)
			18.3 knots (BB-20)	18.3 knots (BB-20)
			18.1 knots (BB-21)	18.1 knots (BB-21)
			18.9 knots (BB-22)	18.9 knots (BB-22)
			18.2 knots (BB-25)	18.2 knots (BB-25)
		Economical	10.0 knots	10.0 knots
	ENGINES	Manufacturer	New York NY (BB-18)	New York NY (BB-18)
			Newport News (BB-19, 22)	Newport News (BB-19, 22)
			Fore R S & E (BB-20)	Fore R S & E (BB-20)
			NY Ship Co. (BB-21, 25)	NY Ship Co. (BB-21, 25)
		Type	Vert. 3-Exp. Recip.	Vert. 3-Exp. Recip.
	HORSEPOWER	Indicated	20,525 (BB-18)	20,525 (BB-18)
			21,350 (BB-19)	21,350 (BB-19)
			18,249 (BB-20)	18,249 (BB-20)
			19,757 (BB-21)	19,757 (BB-21)
			20,572 (BB-22)	20,572 (BB-22)
			17,267 (BB-25)	18,104 (BB-25)
	SCREWS		2	2
	BOILERS	Manufacturer	B & W	B & W
		Type/No.	WT/12	WT/12
	FUEL CAPACITY		2,275 tons coal (BB-18)	2,510 tons coal (BB-18)
			2,400 tons coal (BB-19)	2,446 tons coal (BB-19)
			2,300 tons coal (BB-20)	2,486 tons coal (BB-20)
			2,350 tons coal (BB-21)	2,445 tons coal (BB-21)
			2,250 tons coal (BB-22)	2,420 tons coal (BB-22)
			2,425 tons coal (BB-25)	2,582 tons coal (BB-25)

10: MISSISSIPPI CLASS (BB-23 to BB-24)

Mississippi "(BB-23)"

NAME (HULL NO.)	BUILDER	KEEL LAID	LAUNCHED	COMMISSIONED
MISSISSIPPI "(BB-23)"	W. Cramp	12 May 1904	30 Sep 1905	1 Feb 1908

Authorized 3 Mar 1903. Contract awarded 25 Jan 1904. Sponsored by Miss Mabel C. Money. First Commanding Officer: CAPT John C. Fremont. Rated as COAST BATTLESHIP NO. 23. Placed in comm., in reserve, 1 Aug 1912 at Philadelphia, PA. Placed in full comm.30 Dec 1913. Decomm. 21 Jul 1914 at Newport News, VA. Struck 21 Jul 1914 from the NVR. Trans. 30 Jul 1914 as sale to Greece as KILKIS. Originally was to have been named VASSILEVS GEORGIOS, but was instead named as indicated. Never assigned hull number BB-23. Would have been, had MISSISSIPPI still been on the NVR. Sunk 10 Apr 1941 by German aircraft in Salamis Harbor, Greece.

Mississippi BB-23 — Photograph taken, 1910, anchored in the Mississippi River with the Steamboat Natchez tied up beside her. (Official U.S. Navy Photo)

Mississippi BB-23 — Photograph taken, 3 October 1911, anchored off of New York City, NY.

Mississippi BB-23 — Photograph taken, 14 July 1914, in drydock at the Newport News Shipbuilding & Dry Dock Co., Newport News, VA. Note that the ship was one week away from being decommissioned and transferred to the Greek Navy.

Idaho "(BB-24)"

NAME (HULL NO.)	BUILDER	KEEL LAID	LAUNCHED	COMMISSIONED
IDAHO "(BB-24)"	W. Cramp	12 May 1904	9 Dec 1905	1 Apr 1908

Authorized 3 Mar 1903. Contract awarded 25 Jan 1904. Sponsored by Miss Louise Gooding. First Commanding Officer: CAPT Samuel W. B. Diehl. Rated as COAST BATTLESHIP NO. 24. Placed in comm., in reserve, 27 Oct 1913 at Philadelphia, PA. Placed in full comm. 16 Mar 1914. Decomm. 21 Jul 1914 at Villefranche, France. Struck 30 Jul 1914 from the NVR and trans. as sale to Greece as LEMNOS the same date. Originally was to be named VASILISSA OLGA, but was instead named as indicated. Never assigned hull number BB-24. Would have been, had IDAHO still been on the NVR. Sunk 10 Apr 1941 by German aircraft in Salamis Harbor, Greece.

Idaho BB-24 — Photograph taken, circa 1906, tied up to a pier being fitted out at the William Cramp & Sons, Ship & Engine Building Co., Philadelphia, PA. (U.S. Naval History and Heritage Command Photo)

Idaho BB-24 — Photograph taken, 1909, anchored at an unknown location along the East Coast of the United States. (U.S. Naval History and Heritage Command Photo)

Idaho BB-24 — Photograph taken, 4 October 1912, anchored off of New York City, NY, during a naval review. (U.S. Naval History and Heritage Command Photo)

Class Specifications			As Completed (1908)
HULL	LENGTH	Waterline	375’ 0”
		Overall	382’ 0”
	EXTREME BEAM		77’ 0”
	DISPLACEMENT	Full Load	14,465 tons
		Normal	13,000 tons
	MAXIMUM DRAFT		27’ 0”
	COMPLEMENT	Officers	34
		Enlisted	710
ARMAMENT		Main	(2) twin 12”/45 B.L.R. turrets
			(4) twin 8”/45 B.L.R. turrets
		Secondary	(8) single 7”/45 R.L.R. mounts
			(12) single 3”/50 mounts
			(4) single 6 pdr. saluting
		Torpedo Tubes	(2) 21” submerged
	ARMOR	Belt	
		Top	9”
		Bottom	9”
		Waterline	9”
		Bulkheads	7”
		Deck	
		Forward	3”
		Aft	3”
		Amidships	1.5” – 3”
		12” Gun Turrets	8” – 12”
		8” Gun Turrets	6” – 6.5”
		12” Gun Barbettes	7.5” – 10”
		8” Gun Barbettes	4” – 6”
		Conning Tower	9”
ENGINEERING	SPEED	Maximum	17.1 knots
		Economical	10.0 knots
	ENGINES	Manufacturer	Cramp
		Type	Vert. 3-Exp. Recip.
	HORSEPOWER	Indicated	13,900 (BB-23)
			14,269 (BB-24)
	SCREWS		2
	BOILERS	Manufacturer	B & W
		Type/No.	WT/8
	FUEL CAPACITY		1,824 tons coal

11: SOUTH CAROLINA CLASS (BB-26 to BB-27)

South Carolina (BB-26)

NAME (HULL NO.)	BUILDER	KEEL LAID	LAUNCHED	COMMISSIONED
SOUTH CAROLINA (BB-26)	W. Cramp	18 Dec 1906	11 Jul 1908	1 Mar 1910

Authorized 3 Mar 1905. Contract awarded 21 Jul 1906. Sponsored by Miss Frederica Ansel. First Commanding Officer: CAPT Augustus F. Fechteler. Rated as BATTLESHIP NO. 26. Classified BB-26 on 17 Jul 1920. Decomm. 15 Dec 1921 at Philadelphia, PA. Struck 10 Nov 1923 from the NVR. Demilitarization completed by 12 Jan 1924 in accordance with the terms of the Washington Treaty for Naval Limitations. Partly scrapped and materials sold 24 Apr 1924. Hulk sold 21 Jul 1924. Scrapped.

South Carolina BB-26 — Photograph taken, early October 1911, during the Naval Review at New York City, NY. (Ray D. Bean photo collection)

South Carolina BB-26 — Photograph taken, 27 May 1924, during the second blast at the peak of the explosion at the Philadelphia Navy Yard, Philadelphia, PA. Note that the ship was being used as a test hulk for anti-torpedo bulges.

NAME (HULL NO.)	BUILDER	KEEL LAID	LAUNCHED	COMMISSIONED
MICHIGAN (BB-27)	NY Ship Co.	17 Dec 1906	26 May 1908	4 Jan 1910

Authorized 3 Mar 1905. Contract awarded 20 Jul 1906. Sponsored by Miss Carol B. Newberry. First Commanding Officer: CAPT Nathaniel R. Usher. Rated as BATTLESHIP NO. 27. Placed in limited comm. 6 Aug 1919 at Philadelphia, PA. Placed in ordinary 5 Sep 1919 at Philadelphia, PA. Classified BB-27 on 17 Jul 1920. Recomm. 4 Apr 1921. Decomm. 31 Dec 1921 at Philadelphia, PA. Demilitarization completed by 17 Oct 1923 in accordance with the terms of the Washington Treaty for Naval Limitations. Struck 10 Nov 1923 from the NVR. Hulk sold 23 Jan 1924. Scrapped.

Michigan BB-27 — Photograph taken, 16 November 1909, tied up to a pier at the Philadelphia Navy Yard, Philadelphia, PA. (Ray D. Bean photo collection)

Michigan BB-27 — Photograph taken, 25 September 1916, tied up to a pier at the Philadelphia Navy Yard, Philadelphia, PA, looking aft and next to number two turret. Note the burst gun barrel on the deck and the damage caused by the explosion. The port gun of number two turret blew up while firing at target ship Miantonomoh off Tangier Island in the spring of 1916.

Michigan BB-27 — Photograph taken, 25 September 1916, tied up to a pier at the Philadelphia Navy Yard, Philadelphia, PA, looking at the remains of the port gun of number two 12" turret. The port gun of number two turret blew up while firing at target ship Miantonomoh off Tangier Island in the spring of 1916.

Class Specifications			As Completed (1910)
HULL	LENGTH	Waterline	450' 0"
		Overall	452' 9"
	EXTREME BEAM		80' 2.5"
	DISPLACEMENT	Full Load	17,617 tons
		Normal	16,000 tons
	MAXIMUM DRAFT		27' 1"
	COMPLEMENT	Officers	51
		Enlisted	818
ARMAMENT		Main	(4) twin 12"/45 B.L.R. turrets
		Secondary	(22) single 3"/50 R.F. mounts
			(4) single 3 pdr. (BB-26)
			(2) single 3 pdr. (BB-27)
		Torpedo Tubes	(2) 21" submerged
	ARMOR	Belt	
		Top	11"
		Bottom	9"
		Waterline	10.25"
		Bulkheads	8" – 10"
		Deck	
		Forward	1.5"
		Aft	3"
		Amidships	1.5"
		Turrets	8" – 12"
		Barbettes	8" – 10"
		Conning Tower	12"
ENGINEERING	SPEED	Maximum	18.7 knots (BB-26)
			18.8 knots (BB-27)
		Economical	10.0 knots
	ENGINES	Manufacturer	Cramp (BB-26)
			NY Ship Co. (BB-27)
		Type	Vert. 3-Exp. Recip.
	HORSEPOWER	Indicated	18,357 (BB-26)
			16,517 (BB-27)
	SCREWS		2
	BOILERS	Manufacturer	B & W
		Type/No.	WT/12
	FUEL CAPACITY		2,200 tons coal

12: DELAWARE CLASS (BB-28 to BB-29)

Delaware (BB-28)

NAME (HULL NO.)	BUILDER	KEEL LAID	LAUNCHED	COMMISSIONED
DELAWARE (BB-28)	NNS&DD Co.	11 Nov 1907	6 Feb 1909	4 Apr 1910

Authorized 29 Jun 1906. Contract awarded 6 Aug 1907. Sponsored by Miss Anna Cahall. First Commanding Officer: CAPT Charles A. Gove. Rated as BATTLESHIP NO. 28. Classified BB-28 on 17 Jul 1920. Decomm. 10 Nov 1923 at Boston, MA. Struck 10 Nov 1923 from the NVR. Demilitarization completed by 19 Nov 1923 in accordance with the terms of the Washington Treaty for Naval Limitations. Sold 5 Feb 1924 to the Boston Iron & Metal Co., Baltimore, MD. Scrapped.

Delaware BB-28 — Photograph taken, circa 1909, while underway at high speed during builder's sea trials at an unknown location along the East Coast of the United States. Note that she was flying the National Ensign aft and the Union Jack forward.

Delaware BB-28 — Photograph taken, August 1923, anchored in Hampton Roads, VA. Note the crew's bedding being aired out along the railings of the ship. (Official U.S. Navy Photo)

Delaware BB-28 — Photograph taken, 23 March 1924, while underway being towed from the Boston Navy Yard, Boston, MA, to the Philadelphia Navy Yard, Philadelphia, PA, to be scrapped.

North Dakota (BB-29)

NAME (HULL NO.)	BUILDER	KEEL LAID	LAUNCHED	COMMISSIONED
NORTH DAKOTA (BB-29)	Fore River	16 Dec 1907	10 Nov 1908	11 Apr 1910

Authorized 2 Mar 1907. Contract awarded 6 Aug 1907. Sponsored by Miss Mary Benton. First Commanding Officer: CAPT Charles P. Plunkett. Rated as BATTLESHIP NO. 29. Placed in comm., in reserve, 1 Jul 1915 at Philadelphia, PA. Recomm. 21 Feb 1917. Classified BB-29 on 17 Jul 1920. Decomm. 22 Nov 1923 at Norfolk, VA. Demilitarization completed by 29 May 1924 in accordance with the terms of the Washington Treaty for Naval Limitations and used as a static gunnery target ship. Reclass. UNCLASSIFIED VESSEL. Struck 7 Jan 1931 from the NVR. Sold 16 Mar 1931 to the Union Shipbuilding Co., Baltimore, MD, for $87,706.00. Scrapped.

North Dakota BB-29 — Photograph taken, circa 1911, anchored at an unknown location along the East Coast of the United States. Note that the ship was dressed out in flags and the crew was manning the rails for a special occasion. (Official U.S. Navy Photo)

North Dakota BB-29 — Photograph taken, 7 June 1912, anchored at an unknown location along the East Coast of the United States.

North Dakota BB-29 — Photograph taken, March 1920, while underway at an unknown location in the Atlantic Ocean. (Official U.S. Navy Photo)

Class Specifications			As Completed (1910)
HULL	LENGTH	Waterline	510' 0"
		Overall	518' 9"
	EXTREME BEAM		85' 2.5"
	DISPLACEMENT	Full Load	22,060 tons
		Normal	20,000 tons
	MAXIMUM DRAFT		28' 10"
	COMPLEMENT	Officers	52
		Enlisted	893 (BB-28)
			892 (BB-29)
ARMAMENT		Main	(5) twin 12"/45 B.L.R. turrets
		Secondary	(14) single 5"/51 mounts
			(4) single 3 pdr. saluting
		Torpedo Tubes	(2) 21" submerged
	ARMOR	Belt	9" – 11"
		Bulkheads	10"
		Deck	4"
		Turrets	8" – 12"
		Barbettes	4" – 10"
		Conning Tower	11.5"
ENGINEERING	SPEED	Maximum	21.6 knots (BB-28)
			21.0 knots (BB-29)
		Economical	10.0 knots
	ENGINES	Manufacturer	Newport News (BB-28)
			Fore River (BB-29)
		Type	Vert. 3-Exp. Recip. (BB-28)
			Curtis Turbines (BB-29)
	HORSEPOWER	Indicated	29,529 (BB-28)
		Shaft	32,307 (BB-29)
	SCREWS		2
	BOILERS	Manufacturer	B & W
		Type/No.	WT/14
	FUEL CAPACITY		2,732 tons coal (BB-28)
			2,740 tons coal (BB-29)
	DRIVE		TDD (BB-29)

13: FLORIDA CLASS (BB-30 to BB-31)

Florida (BB-30)

NAME (HULL NO.)	BUILDER	KEEL LAID	LAUNCHED	COMMISSIONED
FLORIDA (BB-30)	New York NY	9 Mar 1909	12 May 1910	15 Sep 1911

Authorized 13 May 1908. Contract awarded 24 Nov 1908. Sponsored by Miss Elizabeth L. Fleming. First Commanding Officer: CAPT Harry S. Knapp. Rated as BATTLESHIP NO. 30. Classified BB-30 on 17 Jul 1920. Placed in reduced comm. 25 Jul 1924 for modernization at Boston, MA. Rebuilt at Boston Navy Yard (1 Apr 1925 – 1 Nov 1926). Placed in full comm. 24 Oct 1926. Decomm. 16 Feb 1931 at Philadelphia, PA. Demilitarized and struck 6 Apr 1931 from the NVR. Scrapped at the Philadelphia Navy Yard. Scrapping being completed 6 Apr 1931. Scrap materials sold 30 Sep 1932.

Florida BB-30 — Photograph taken, circa 1912, anchored at New York City, NY, during a naval review. (Ray D. Bean photo collection)

Florida BB-30 — Photograph taken, 8 June 1913, anchored at an unknown location along the East Coast of the United States. (Official U.S. Navy Photo)

Florida BB-30 — Photograph taken, February 1930, anchored at an unknown location along the East Coast of the United States. (Official U.S. Navy Photo)

Utah (BB-31)

NAME (HULL NO.)	BUILDER	KEEL LAID	LAUNCHED	COMMISSIONED
UTAH (BB-31)	NY Ship Co.	15 Mar 1909	23 Dec 1909	31 Aug 1911

Authorized 13 May 1908. Contract awarded 24 Nov 1908. Sponsored by Miss Mary A. Spry. First Commanding Officer: CAPT William S. Benson. Rated as BATTLESHIP NO. 31. Classified BB-31 on 17 Jul 1920. Placed in reduced comm. 31 Oct 1926 for modernization at Boston, MA. Rebuilt at Boston Navy Yard (August 1926–28 Oct 1927). Placed in full comm. August 1928. Placed in reduced comm. 16 Feb 1931 for conversion to a remote controlled target ship at Norfolk, VA. Converted to MISCELLANEOUS AUXILIARY (1930–1932). Reclass. AG-16 on 1 Jul 1931. Placed in full comm. 1 Apr 1932. Sunk 7 Dec 1941 by Japanese aircraft at Pearl Harbor, HI. Placed in ordinary 29 Dec 1941. Found to be beyond salvage and placed out of comm., not in service 5 Sep 1944. Struck 13 Nov 1944 from the NVR. Sunken hulk maintained as a memorial at Pearl Harbor, HI.

Utah BB-31 — Photograph taken, September 1911, tied up to a pier at the New York Navy Yard, Brooklyn, NY, shortly after commissioning. (Ray D. Bean photo collection)

Utah BB-31 — Photograph taken, circa 1918, anchored at an unknown location along the East Coast of the United States. Note her unusual camouflage pattern painted on the hull and the triangular baffles attached to the masts. These were intended to confuse enemy range finders. (Official U.S. Navy Photo)

Utah BB-31 — Photograph taken, circa 1928, while underway at an unknown location along the East Coast of the United States following her modernization by the Boston Navy Yard, Boston, MA. (Official U.S. Navy Photo)

Utah AG-16 — Photograph taken, 10 December 1936, while underway at an unknown location in the Pacific Ocean. Note the timbers arranged on her weather decks to cushion the impact of water-filled bombs. (Official U.S. Navy Photo)

Class Specifications			As Completed (1911)	Operational Condition as of 1929
HULL	LENGTH	Waterline	510' 0"	510' 0"
		Overall	521' 6"	521' 6"
	EXTREME BEAM		88' 2.5"	106' 0"
	DISPLACEMENT	Full Load	23,033 tons	24,800 tons
		Normal	21,825 tons	23,700 tons
	MAXIMUM DRAFT		30' 1"	28' 8"
	COMPLEMENT	Officers	60	81 (BB-30)
				64 (BB-31)
		Enlisted	941	1,090
ARMAMENT		Main	(5) twin 12"/45 B.L.R. turrets	(5) twin 12"/45 B.L.R. turrets
		Secondary	(16) single 5"/51 mounts	(12) single 5"/51 mounts
			(4) single 3 pdr.	(8) single 3"/50 A.A. mounts
				(4) single 6 pdr. saluting (BB-30)
				(4) single 3 pdr. saluting (BB-31)
		Torpedo Tubes	(2) 21" submerged	None
	ARMOR	Belt	3" – 11"	3" – 11"
		Deck	3"	3"
		Turrets	8" – 12"	8" – 12"
		Barbettes	4" – 10"	4" – 10"
		Conning Tower	11.5"	11.5"
	AIRCRAFT	Number	None	2
		Catapults	None	(1) top of #3 turret
ENGINEERING	SPEED	Maximum	22.1 knots (BB-30)	22.1 knots (BB-30)
			21.0 knots (BB-31)	21.0 knots (BB-31)
		Economical	10.0 knots	10.0 knots
	ENGINES	Manufacturer	New York NY (BB-30)	New York NY (BB-30)
			NY Ship Co. (BB-31)	NY Ship Co. (BB-31)
		Type	Parsons Turbines	Parsons Turbines
	HORSEPOWER	Shaft	31,810 (BB-30)	41,810 (BB-30)
			28,136 (BB-31)	28,136 (BB-31)
	SCREWS		4	4
	BOILERS	Manufacturer	B & W	White-Forster
		Type/No.	WT/12	WT/4
	FUEL CAPACITY		2,500 tons coal (BB-30)	2,560 tons oil (BB-30)
			2,520 tons coal (BB-31)	2,581 tons oil (BB-31)
	DRIVE		TD	TD

14: WYOMING CLASS (BB-32 to BB-33)

Wyoming (BB-32)

NAME (HULL NO.)	BUILDER	KEEL LAID	LAUNCHED	COMMISSIONED
WYOMING (BB-32)	W. Cramp	9 Feb 1910	25 May 1911	25 Sep 1912

Authorized 3 Mar 1909. Contract awarded 14 Oct 1909. Sponsored by Miss Dorothy E. Knight. First Commanding Officer: CAPT Frederick L. Chapin. Rated as BATTLESHIP NO. 32. Classified BB-32 on 17 Jul 1920. Placed in reduced comm. 1926 for modernization at Philadelphia, PA. Rebuilt at Philadelphia Navy Yard (1926 – 2 Nov 1927). Placed in full comm. 1927. Placed in reduced comm. 1 Jan 1931 for conversion to a gunnery training ship at the Norfolk Navy Yard. Reclass. AG-17 on 1 Jul 1931. After Pearl Harbor, it was seriously considered to reconvert this ship back to a full Battleship, but the idea was dropped due to cost. Decomm. 1 Aug 1947 at Norfolk, VA. Struck 16 Sep 1947 from the NVR. Sold 30 Oct 1947 to Lipsett Div., Liguria Bros., New York City, NY. Scrapped.

Wyoming BB-32 — Photograph taken, circa 1912, while underway at high speed during builder's sea trials at an unknown location along the East Coast of the United States. Note the 5"/51 caliber anti-destroyer gun mount at the extreme stern of the ship. The Wyoming, New York and Nevada classes were designed and originally armed with this weapon.

Wyoming BB-32 — Photograph taken, circa 1913, while underway going under the Brooklyn Bridge on the way to the New York Navy Yard, Brooklyn, NY. (Ray D. Bean photo collection)

Wyoming BB-32 — Photograph taken, 26 July 1919, while underway going through the Panama Canal's Gaillard Cut on her way to San Diego, CA. (Official U.S. Navy Photo)

Wyoming AG-17 — Photograph taken, 31 March 1931, while being converted into a training ship by the Philadelphia Navy Yard, Philadelphia, PA. Note the partially dismantled turret. (Official U.S. Navy Photo)

Wyoming AG-17 — Photograph taken, 31 March 1931, while being converted into a training ship by the Philadelphia Navy Yard, Philadelphia, PA. Note the partially dismantled turret. (Official U.S. Navy Photo)

Wyoming AG-17 — Photograph taken, June 1942, anchored in Chesapeake Bay, VA. Note her unusual camouflage pattern. (Official U.S. Navy Photo)

Wyoming AG-17 — Photograph taken, 17 June 1943, while underway in Chesapeake Bay, VA. (Official U.S. Navy Photo)

Wyoming AG-17 — Photograph taken, 30 April 1945, while underway in Hampton Roads, VA. Note that her 12-inch turrets had been removed and replaced with twin 5-inch mounts. (Official U.S. Navy Photo)

Wyoming AG-17 — Photograph taken, 30 April 1945, while underway in Hampton Roads, VA. Note that her 12-inch turrets had been removed and replaced with twin 5-inch mounts and newer models of fire control radars were installed. (Official U.S. Navy Photo)

Wyoming AG-17 — Photograph taken, 30 April 1945, while underway in Hampton Roads, VA. Note that her 12-inch turrets had been removed and replaced with twin 5-inch mounts and newer models of fire control radars were installed. (Official U.S. Navy Photo)

Arkansas (BB-33)

NAME (HULL NO.)	BUILDER	KEEL LAID	LAUNCHED	COMMISSIONED
ARKANSAS (BB-33)	NY Ship Co.	25 Jan 1910	14 Jan 1911	17 Sep 1912

Authorized 3 Mar 1909. Contract awarded 25 Sep 1909. Sponsored by Miss Mary L. Macon. First Commanding Officer: CAPT Roy C. Smith. Rated as BATTLESHIP NO. 33. Classified BB-33 on 17 Jul 1920. Placed in reduced comm. 1925 for modernization at Philadelphia, PA. Rebuilt at Philadelphia Navy Yard (1 Sep 1925 – 21 Nov 1926). Placed in full comm. 21 Nov 1926. Employed as a target ship in July 1946 for the "Operation Crossroads" Atomic Bomb tests at Bikini Atoll, Marshall Islands. Sunk 25 Jul 1946 as a result of Atomic Bomb test "Baker" at Bikini Atoll and was decomm. there the same date. Struck 15 Aug 1946 from the NVR.

Arkansas BB-33 — Photograph taken, circa 1912, while underway at an unknown location along the East Coast of the United States shortly after her commissioning. (Ray D. Bean photo collection)

Arkansas BB-33 — Photograph taken, 21 August 1923, anchored in Hampton Roads, VA. (Official U.S. Navy Photo)

Arkansas BB-33 — Photograph taken, February 1929, while underway in the Caribbean Sea. Note that during her modernization, the aft cage mast was removed and replaced with a low tripod mast and a single stack was substituted for the original pair.

Arkansas BB-33 — Photograph taken, 27 June 1942, while underway in the Elizabeth River during an overhaul by the Norfolk Navy Yard, Portsmouth, VA. (Ray D. Bean photo collection)

Arkansas BB-33 — Photograph taken, 5 November 1944, while underway in Boston Harbor, Boston, MA, following repairs and alterations by the Boston Navy Yard, Boston, MA. Note that she wore a Measure 31a/7B camouflage pattern. (Official U.S. Navy Photo)

Arkansas BB-33 — Photograph taken, 1 January 1945, anchored in San Pedro Harbor, CA. Note that she wore a Measure 21 camouflage pattern. (Official U.S. Navy Photo)

Arkansas BB-33 — Photograph taken, 1 January 1945, anchored in San Pedro Harbor, CA. Note that she wore a Measure 21 camouflage pattern. (Official U.S. Navy Photo)

Class Specifications			As Completed (1912)	Operational Condition as of 1929
HULL	LENGTH	Waterline	554' 0"	554' 0"
		Overall	562' 0"	562' 0"
	EXTREME BEAM		93' 2.5"	106' 0"
	DISPLACEMENT	Full Load	27,243 tons	29,000 tons
		Normal	26,000 tons	27,900 tons
	MAXIMUM DRAFT		29' 7"	28' 6"
	COMPLEMENT	Officers	62	77 (BB-32)
				65 (BB-33)
		Enlisted	976 (BB-32)	1,186 (BB-32)
			978 (BB-33)	1,177 (BB-33)
ARMAMENT		Main	(6) twin 12"/50 B.L.R. turrets	(6) twin 12"/50 B.L.R. turrets
		Secondary	(21) single 5"/51 mounts	(16) single 5"/51 mounts
			(4) single 3 pdr. saluting	(8) single 3"/50 AA mounts
				(4) single 6 pdr. saluting (BB-32)
				(4) single 3 pdr. saluting (BB-33)
		Torpedo Tubes	(2) 21" submerged	None
	ARMOR	Belt	9" – 11"	9" – 11"
		Deck	3"	3"
		Turrets	9" – 12"	9" – 12"
		Barbettes	4.5" – 11"	4.5" – 12"
		Conning Tower	11.5"	11.5"
	AIRCRAFT	Number	None	2
		Catapults	None	(1) top of #3 turret
ENGINEERING	SPEED	Maximum	21.2 knots (BB-32)	21.2 knots (BB-32)
			21.1 knots (BB-33)	21.1 knots (BB-33)
		Economical	20.0 knots	20.0 knots
	ENGINES	Manufacturer	Cramp (BB-32)	Cramp (BB-32)
			NY Ship Co. (BB-33)	NY Ship Co. (BB-33)
		Type	Parsons Direct Drive	Parsons Direct Drive
			Turbines	Turbines
	HORSEPOWER	Shaft	34,956 (BB-32)	28,136 (BB-32)
			29,319 (BB-33)	29,319 (BB-33)
	SCREWS		4	4
	BOILERS	Manufacturer	B & W	White-Forster
		Type/No.	WT/12	WT/4
	FUEL CAPACITY		2,641 tons coal (BB-32)	5,278 tons oil
			2,691 tons coal (BB-33)	
	DRIVE		TDD	TDD

15: NEW YORK CLASS (BB-34 to BB-35)

New York (BB-34)

NAME (HULL NO.)	BUILDER	KEEL LAID	LAUNCHED	COMMISSIONED
NEW YORK (BB-34)	New York NY	11 Sep 1911	30 Dec 1912	15 Apr 1914

Authorized 24 Jun 1910. Contract awarded 1 May 1911. Sponsored by Miss Elsie Calder. First Commanding Officer: CAPT Thomas S. Rodgers. Rated as BATTLESHIP NO. 34. Classified BB-34 on 17 Jul 1920. Placed in reduced comm. 1926 for modernization at Norfolk, VA. Rebuilt at Norfolk Navy Yard (1926 – 10 Oct 1927). Placed in full comm. 1927. Employed as a target ship in July 1946 for the "Operation Crossroads" Atomic Bomb tests at Bikini Atoll, Marshall Islands. Decomm. 29 Aug 1946 at Kwajalein Atoll, Marshall Islands. Sunk 8 Jul 1948 as a target by aircraft and naval gunfire 40 miles Southwest of Pearl Harbor, HI. Struck 13 Jul 1948 from the NVR.

New York BB-34 — Photo taken, 1 December 1911, while under construction at the New York Navy Yard, Brooklyn, NY.

New York BB-34 — Photo taken, 1914, while underway at high speed during builder's sea trials at an unknown location along the East Coast of the United States. (Official U.S. Navy Photo)

New York BB-34 — Photo taken, October 1924, anchored in Hampton Roads, VA. (Official U.S. Navy Photo)

New York BB-34 — Photograph taken, 10 April 1927, while undergoing an extensive rebuilding at the Norfolk Navy Yard, Portsmouth, VA. (Ray D. Bean photo collection)

New York BB-34 — Photograph taken, 17 October 1929, anchored in Hampton Roads, VA. Note her new appearance since undergoing extensive rebuilding by the Norfolk Navy Yard, Portsmouth, VA. (Official U.S. Navy Photo)

New York BB-34 — Photograph taken, 12 August 1942, while underway in the Elizabeth River following an overhaul, additional modernization and modifications by the Norfolk Navy Yard, Portsmouth, VA. Note that she wore a Measure 12 Modified camouflage pattern. (Official U.S. Navy Photo)

New York BB-34 — Photograph taken, 13 June 1944, while underway on a midshipmen cruise at an unknown location along the East Coast of the United States. Note that she wore a Measure 22 camouflage pattern. (Official U.S. Navy Photo)

New York BB-34 — Photograph taken, 14 November 1944, while underway off of Hampton Roads, VA. Note that she wore a Measure 31a/8B camouflage pattern. (Official U.S. Navy Photo)

Texas (BB-35)

NAME (HULL NO.)	BUILDER	KEEL LAID	LAUNCHED	COMMISSIONED
TEXAS (BB-35)	NNS&DD Co.	17 Apr 1911	18 May 1912	12 Mar 1914

Authorized 24 Jun 1910. Contract awarded 17 Dec 1910. Sponsored by Miss Claudia Lyon. First Commanding Officer: CAPT Albert W. Grant. Rated as BATTLESHIP NO. 35. Classified BB-35 on 17 Jul 1920. Placed in reduced comm. 1925 for modernization at Norfolk, VA. Rebuilt at Norfolk Navy Yard (1 Aug 1925 – 23 Nov 1926). Placed in full comm. 1926. Decomm. 21 Apr 1948 at San Jacinto State Park, Houston, TX, and presented to the State of Texas as a memorial/museum ship the same date. Struck 30 Apr 1948 from the NVR. Custody trans. 1 Sep 1983 to the Texas Parks and Wildlife Department. By the early 1980's, leaks from above and major flooding below made it evident that the ship needed drydocking. The approved FY 1987 Department of Defense budget contained a clause allocating $5,080,500.00 from the Navy's operating funds for the purpose of drydocking the ship. Efforts on 13 Dec 1988 to float the ship, with 7 tugs assisting, finally bore fruit after 8 hours. The tow to Galveston, TX, for drydocking on the same date, took 10 hours and was a rapid race against increased flooding caused by breaking her free from her 40 year berth, and the movement of the hull through the water. It did not help the towing ships that TEXAS's rudder was stuck 15 deg. to starboard. Besides replacing 3,000 sq. ft. of main deck plating, 1,100 sq. ft. of inner bottom plating in the engine room bilges, 14,100 sq. ft. of blister plating and 43,000 leaking rivets, (10) quad 40-mm mounts, removed from the recently reactived MISSOURI (BB-63), were added to the ship in lieu of (4) quad 1.1" guns originally mounted on the ship. Refloated in September 1989 and remained alongside at Galveston until February 1990 when she was redocked again for repairs of leaks and bottom touch up. Undocked March 1990. Remained at a temporary berth in the Houston Ship Channel at a pier at Green Bayou for more topside repairs. Returned in September 1990 to her permanent berth at San Jacinto, TX, where she remains berthed. Total cost of the 21 month overhaul was $18.0 million.

Texas BB-35 — Photograph taken, 27 October 1913, while underway at high speed, making 20.033 knots on builder's sea trials at an unknown location along the East Coast of the United States. (Official U.S. Navy Photo)

Texas BB-35 — Photograph taken, March 1919, while underway at an unknown location along the East Coast of the United States. Note the British-built Sopwith Camel sitting on top of the number two turret. (Official U.S. Navy Photo)

Texas BB-35 — Photograph taken, circa 1920–1923, anchored at an unknown location in the Pacific Ocean. (Official U.S. Navy Photo)

Texas BB-35 — Photograph taken, 12 February 1930, anchored at Coco Solo, Panama, Canal Zone. Note her new appearance since undergoing extensive rebuilding by the Norfolk Navy Yard, Portsmouth, VA. (Official U.S. Navy Photo)

Texas BB-35 — Photograph taken, 8 June 1940, anchored off of Annapolis, MD, picking up midshipmen from the U.S. Naval Academy for their summer cruise.

Texas BB-35 — Photograph taken, 15 March 1943, while underway in the Elizabeth River following an overhaul by the Norfolk Navy Yard, Portsmouth, VA. Note that she wore a Measure 22 camouflage pattern. (Official U.S. Navy Photo)

Texas BB-35 — Photograph taken, 21 December 1943, while underway about 60 miles east of Virginia Beach, VA, in the Atlantic Ocean. Note that she wore a Measure 22 camouflage pattern and that this was her final wartime appearance. (Official U.S. Navy Photo)

Texas BB-35 — Photograph taken, February 1945, while underway among numerous ships off of Iwo Jima, delivering support and "call fire" to the troops ashore. (Official U.S. Navy Photo)

Texas BB-35 — Photograph taken, circa late 1945, while underway at an unknown along the West Coast of the United States. (Official U.S. Navy Photo)

Texas BB-35 — Photograph taken, 25 May 2005, moored as a museum and memorial at San Jacinto State Park at La Porte, TX. (George R. Schneider photo collection)

Class Specifications			As Completed (1914)	Operational Condition as of 1929
HULL	LENGTH	Waterline	565' 0"	565' 0"
		Overall	573' 0"	573' 0"
	EXTREME BEAM		95' 2.5"	106' 1"
	DISPLACEMENT	Full Load	28,367 tons	30,000 tons
		Normal	27,000 tons	28,700 tons
	MAXIMUM DRAFT		29' 7"	28' 7"
	COMPLEMENT	Officers	58	83 (BB-34)
				87 (BB-35)
		Enlisted	994	1,208
ARMAMENT		Main	(5) twin 14"/45 B.L.R. turrets	(5) twin 14"/45 B.L.R. turrets
		Secondary	(21) single 5"/51 mounts	(16) single 5"/51 mounts
			(4) single 3 pdr. saluting	(8) single 3"/50 AA mounts
				(4) single 3 pdr. saluting
		Torpedo Tubes	(4) 21" submerged	None
	ARMOR	Belt	6" – 12"	6" – 12"
		Bulkheads	9" – 11"	9" – 11"
		Deck	3"	3"
		Turrets	8" – 14"	8" – 14"
		Barbettes	5" – 12"	5" – 12"
		Conning Tower	12"	12"
	AIRCRAFT	Number	None	2 – 3
		Catapults	None	(1) top of #3 turret
ENGINEERING	SPEED	Maximum	21.5 knots (BB-34)	20.2 knots (BB-34)
			21.1 knots (BB-35)	19.8 knots (BB-35)
		Economical	20.0 knots	20.0 knots
	ENGINES	Manufacturer	New York NY (BB-34)	New York NY (BB-34)
			Newport News (BB-35)	Newport News (BB-35)
		Type	Vert. 3-Exp. Recip.	Vert. 3-Exp. Recip.
	HORSEPOWER	Indicated	29,687 (BB-34)	29,687 (BB-34)
			28,373 (BB-35)	28,373 (BB-35)
	SCREWS		2	2
	BOILERS	Manufacturer	B & W	Bureau Express
		Type/No.	WT/12	WT/6
	FUEL CAPACITY		2,850 tons coal (BB-34)	5,192 tons oil
			2,892 tons coal (BB-35)	

16: NEVADA CLASS (BB-36 to BB-37)

Nevada (BB-36)

NAME (HULL NO.)	BUILDER	KEEL LAID	LAUNCHED	COMMISSIONED
NEVADA (BB-36)	Fore River	4 Nov 1912	11 Jul 1914	11 Mar 1916

Authorized 4 Mar 1911. Contract awarded 22 Jan 1912. Sponsored by Miss Eleanor A. Seibert. First Commanding Officer: CAPT William S. Sims. Rated as BATTLESHIP NO. 36. Classified BB-36 on 17 Jul 1920. Placed in reduced comm. 17 Sep 1927 for modernization at Norfolk, VA. Rebuilt at Norfolk Navy Yard (27 Sep 1927–26 Nov 1929). Re-engined with turbines from the scrapped NORTH DAKOTA (ex BB-29) at the same time. Placed in full comm. 9 Jan 1930. Employed as a target ship in July 1946 for the "Operation Crossroads" Atomic Bomb tests at Bikini Atoll, Marshall Islands. Decomm. 29 Aug 1946 at Pearl Harbor, HI. Struck 12 Aug 1948 from the NVR. Sunk 30 Jul 1948 as a target by gunfire from a destroyer, a cruiser, and the USS IOWA (BB-61), and finally by an aerial torpedo amidships, 65 miles southwest of Pearl Harbor, HI.

Nevada BB-36 — Photograph taken, November 1915, while underway at high speed, making 22.5 knots during builder's sea trials off of Rockland, ME. (Ray D. Bean photo collection)

Nevada BB-36 — Photograph taken, 18 September 1916, while underway at an unknown location along the East Coast of the United States.

Nevada BB-36 — Photograph taken, 6 April 1937, while underway at high speed at an unknown location in the Pacific Ocean. Note that her and her forward turrets were trained to starboard. (Official U.S. Navy Photo)

Nevada BB-36 — Photograph taken, 7 December 1941, grounded in shallow waters just off Waipio Point, HI. Note that she wore a Measure 1/Measure 5, False Bow Wave, camouflage pattern. (Official U.S. Navy Photo)

Nevada BB-36 — Photograph taken, 17 July 1943, while underway at an unknown location in the Pacific Ocean on her way to the Panama Canal. Note that she wore a Measure 21 camouflage pattern. (Official U.S. Navy Photo)

Nevada BB-36 — Photographs taken, 23 August 1943, while underway in the Elizabeth River following further modernization by the Norfolk Navy Yard, Portsmouth, VA. Note that she wore a Measure 22 camouflage pattern. (Official U.S. Navy Photo)

Nevada BB-36 — Photograph taken, 17 September 1944, while underway about 35 miles east of New York City, NY, in the Atlantic Ocean. Note that she wore a Measure 22 camouflage pattern. (Official U.S. Navy Photo)

Nevada BB-36 — Photograph taken, 8 November 1944, while underway in the Elizabeth River following an overhaul by the Norfolk Navy Yard, Portsmouth, VA. Note that she wore a Measure 31a/6B camouflage pattern. (Official U.S. Navy Photo)

Nevada BB-36 — Photograph taken, 2 December 1945, in Dry Dock No. 1 at the Pearl Harbor Naval Shipyard, Pearl Harbor, HI. (Ray D. Bean photo collection)

Oklahoma (BB-37)

NAME (HULL NO.)	BUILDER	KEEL LAID	LAUNCHED	COMMISSIONED
OKLAHOMA (BB-37)	NY Ship Corp.	26 Oct 1912	23 Mar 1914	2 May 1916

Authorized 4 Mar 1911. Contract awarded 22 Jan 1912. Sponsored by Miss Lorena J. Cruce. First Commanding Officer: CAPT Roger Welles. Rated as BATTLESHIP NO. 37. Classified BB-37 on 17 Jul 1920. Placed in reduced comm. 16 Sep 1927 for modernization at Philadelphia, PA. Rebuilt at Philadelphia Navy Yard (16 Sep 1927–15 Jul 1929). Placed in full comm. 15 Jul 1929. Capsized and sank 7 Dec 1941 by Japanese aircraft torpedoes and bombs at Pearl Harbor, HI. Raised. Surveyed and found to be beyond economical repair. Decomm. 1 Sep 1944 at Pearl Harbor, HI. Struck 22 Nov 1944 from the NVR. Sold 5 Dec 1946 to the Moore Drydock Co., Oakland, CA, for $180,000.00 for scrapping. Sunk 17 May 1947, while under tow to Oakland, 540 miles east of Pearl Harbor, HI.

Oklahoma BB-37 — Photograph taken, circa 1921, while underway at an unknown location in the Pacific Ocean firing a 14" broadside. (Official U.S. Navy Photo)

Oklahoma BB-37 — Photograph taken, 10 September 1927, tied up to a pier at an unknown location on the East Coast of the United States, just prior to entering the Philadelphia Navy Yard, Philadelphia, PA, for an extensive rebuilding.

Oklahoma BB-37 — Photograph taken, circa 1928, in drydock undergoing an extensive rebuilding by the Philadelphia Navy Yard, Philadelphia, PA. (Ray D. Bean photo collection)

Oklahoma BB-37 — Photograph taken, circa 1930, while underway at an unknown location in the Pacific Ocean leading a line of battleships. Note that all of her turrets were trained 90 degrees to starboard. (Official U.S. Navy Photo)

Oklahoma BB-37 — Photograph taken, June 1936, while underway at an unknown location in the Atlantic Ocean during a midshipmen cruise to Europe. (Official U.S. Navy Photo)

Oklahoma BB-37 — Photograph taken, 29 March 1943, under salvage at Pearl Harbor, HI. She had capsized and sunk during the Japanese attack on 7 December 1941 at Pearl Harbor, HI. Note that at this point, the ship was righted to about 30 degrees. (Official U.S. Navy Photo)

Class Specifications			As Completed (1916)	Operational Condition as of 1935
HULL	LENGTH	Waterline	575' 0"	575' 0"
		Overall	583' 0"	583' 0"
	EXTREME BEAM		95' 2.5"	107' 11"
	DISPLACEMENT	Full Load	28,400 tons	31,961 tons (BB-36)
				32,338 tons (BB-37)
		Normal	27,500 tons	29,000 tons
	MAXIMUM DRAFT		29' 7" (BB-36)	32' 6"
			29' 7.5" (BB-37)	
	COMPLEMENT	Officers	55	79 (BB-36)
				88 (BB-37)
		Enlisted	809	1,285 (BB-36)
				1,641 (BB-37)
		Marines	75	None
ARMAMENT		Main	(2) triple 14"/45 B.L.R. turrets	(2) triple 14"/45 B.L.R. turrets
			(2) twin 14"/45 B.L.R. turrets	(2) twin 14"/45 B.L.R. turrets
		Secondary	(21) single 5"/51 mounts	(12) single 5"/51 mounts
			(4) single 3"/50 AA mounts	(8) single 5"/25 AA mounts
			(4) single 3 pdr. saluting	(4) single 6 pdr. saluting (BB-36)
				(4) single 3 pdr. saluting (BB-37)
		Torpedo Tubes	(2) 21" submerged	None
	ARMOR	Belt	8" – 13.5"	13.5"
		Bulkheads	8" – 13"	8" – 13"
		Deck	2" – 3"	2" – 3"
		Triple Turrets	9" – 18"	9" – 18"
		Twin Turrets	9" – 16"	9" – 16"
		Barbettes	13"	13"
		Conning Tower	16"	16"
	AIRCRAFT	Number	None	3
		Catapults	None	(1) top of #3 turret
				(1) quarter deck aft
ENGINEERING	SPEED	Maximum	20.5 knots (BB-36)	20.3 knots (BB-36)
			20.6 knots (BB-37)	19.7 knots (BB-37)
		Economical	10.0 knots	10.0 knots
	ENGINES	Manufacturer	Curtis (BB-36)	Parsons (BB-36)
			NY Ship Corp. (BB-37)	NY Ship Corp. (BB-37)
		Type	Geared Turbines (BB-36)	Geared Turbines (BB-36)
			Vert. 3-Exp. Recip. (BB-37)	Vert. 3-Exp. Recip. (BB-37)
	HORSEPOWER	Shaft	23,312 (BB-36)	31,214 (BB-36)
		Indicated	21,703 (BB-37)	23,300 (BB-37)
	SCREWS		2	2
	BOILERS	Manufacturer	Yarrow (BB-36)	Bureau Express
			B & W (BB-37)	
		Type/No.	WT/12	WT/6
	FUEL CAPACITY		2,000 tons oil	5,013 tons oil
	DRIVE		TRD (BB-36)	TRD (BB-36)

17: PENNSYLVANIA CLASS (BB-38 to BB-39)

Pennsylvania (BB-38)

NAME (HULL NO.)	BUILDER	KEEL LAID	LAUNCHED	COMMISSIONED
PENNSYLVANIA (BB-38)	NNS&DD Co.	27 Oct 1913	16 Mar 1915	12 Jun 1916

Authorized 22 Aug 1912. Contract awarded 28 Feb 1913. Sponsored by Miss Elizabeth Kolb. First Commanding Officer: CAPT Henry B. Wilson. Rated as BATTLESHIP NO. 38. Classified BB-38 on 17 Jul 1920. Placed in reduced comm. 1 Jun 1929 for modernization at Philadelphia, PA. Rebuilt at Philadelphia Navy Yard (1 June 1929 – 8 May 1931). Re-engined at the same time with turbines originally intended for the sunk WASHINGTON (BB-47). Placed in full comm. 8 May 1931. Employed as a target ship in July 1946 for the "Operation Crossroads" Atomic Bomb tests at Bikini Atoll, Marshall Islands. Decomm. 29 Aug 1946 at Kwajalein Atoll, Marshall Islands. Struck 19 Feb 1948 from the NVR. Scuttled 10 Nov 1948 off Kwajalein Atoll.

Pennsylvania BB-38 — Photograph taken, 16 March 1915, on the day of her launching. Note the teak wood backing on the hull just in back of the forward launch cradle cables. During outfitting, the ships' side armor will be bolted to the hull through the teak wood. Also note the starboard side submerged 21" torpedo tube opening just below the teak wood.

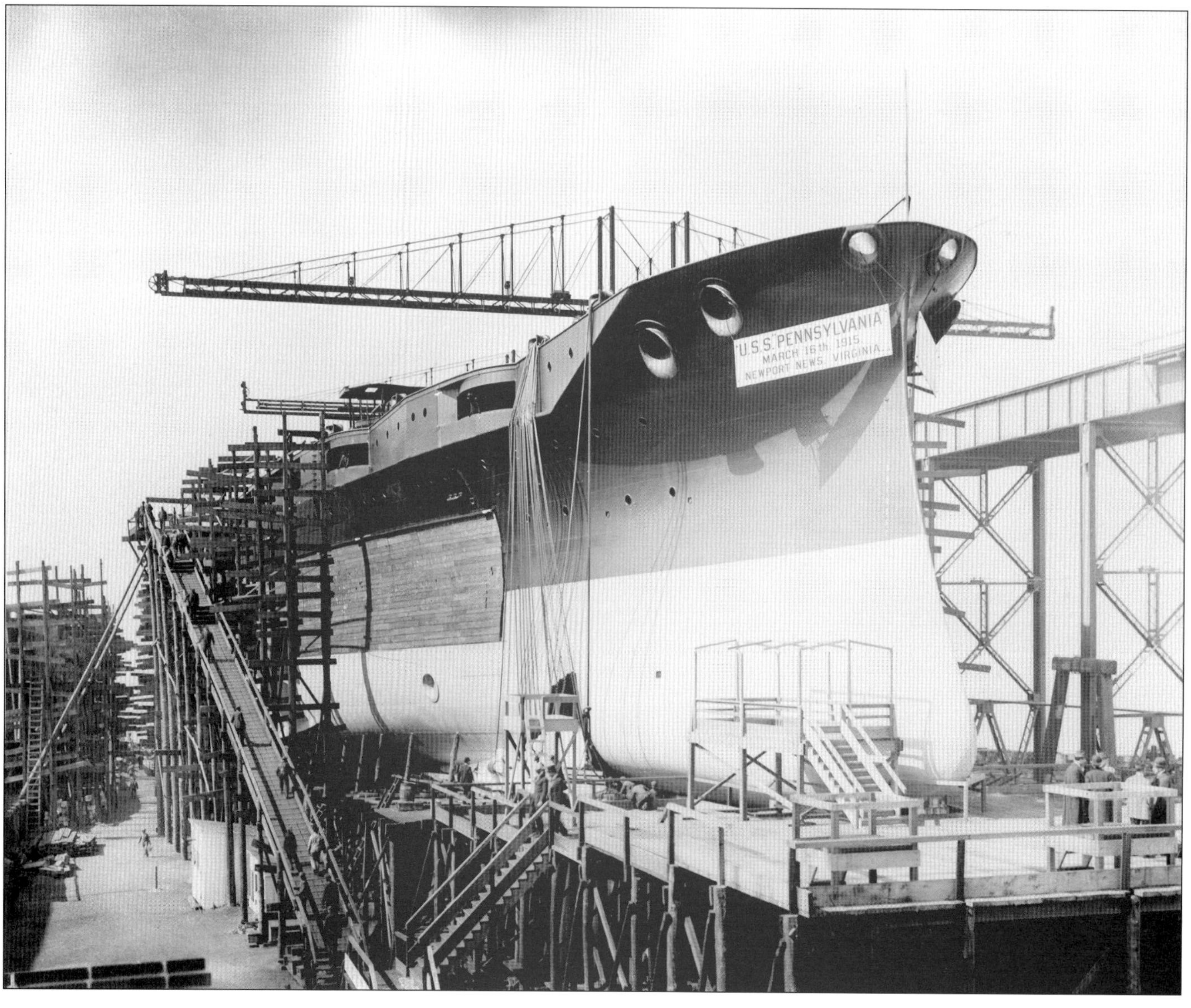

Pennsylvania BB-38 — Photograph taken, circa 1915–1916, tied up to a pier at the Newport News Shipbuilding & Dry Dock Co., Newport News, VA, being fitted out. (Official U.S. Navy Photo)

Pennsylvania BB-38 — Photograph taken, 2 December 1918, anchored off of Tompkinsville, NY, getting ready to escort SS George Washington with President Woodrow Wilson onboard to Brest, France.

Pennsylvania BB-38 — Photograph taken, November 1935, while underway at an unknown location along the West Coast of the United States. (Official U.S. Navy Photo)

Pennsylvania BB-38 — Photograph taken, 2 March 1942, tied up to a pier in San Francisco, CA. Note the new shields on the AA guns amidships and the machine gun position just below the guns of the number four turret. Also note that the light AA armament was manned and ready, even though the ship was tied up to a pier. (Official U.S. Navy Photo)

Pennsylvania BB-38 — Photograph taken, 1 February 1943, while underway in San Francisco Bay, CA, following an overhaul by the Bethlehem Steel Co., Shipbuilding Division, San Francisco, CA. Note that she wore a Measure 21 camouflage pattern. (Official U.S. Navy Photo)

Pennsylvania BB-38 — Photograph taken, summer 1943, while underway with the crew relaxing from battle stations during operations in the Aleutian Islands, AK. (Ray D. Bean photo collection)

Pennsylvania BB-38 — Photographs taken, 1 August 1943, while underway off of Port Townsend, WA, following a refit by Puget Sound Navy Yard, Bremerton, WA. Note that she wore a Measure 21 camouflage pattern. (Official U.S. Navy Photo)

Pennsylvania BB-38 — Photograph taken, 8 June 1945, while underway in San Francisco Bay, CA, during an overhaul by the San Francisco Naval Shipyard, San Francisco, CA. Note that she wore a Measure 21 camouflage pattern. (Official U.S. Navy Photo)

Arizona (BB-39)

NAME (HULL NO.)	BUILDER	KEEL LAID	LAUNCHED	COMMISSIONED
ARIZONA (BB-39)	New York NY	16 Mar 1914	19 Jun 1915	27 Oct 1916

Authorized 4 Mar 1913. Contract awarded 24 Jun 1913. Sponsored by Miss Esther Ross. First Commanding Officer: CAPT John D. McDonald. Rated as BATTLESHIP NO. 39. Classified BB-39 on 17 Jul 1920. Placed in reduced comm. 4 May 1929 for modernization at Norfolk, VA. Rebuilt at Norfolk Navy Yard. Placed in full comm. 1 Mar 1931. Blew up and sunk 7 Dec 1941 by Japanese aircraft torpedoes and bombs at Pearl Harbor, HI. Placed in ordinary 29 Dec 1941. Struck 1 Dec 1942 from the NVR. Her topside superstructure was removed and scrapped and turret # 1 with guns remained in place. Her after turrets with their guns were removed and became the famous "Oahu turrets". The guns from turret # 2 went to Nevada (BB-36) for use in turret # 1 during her late 1944 overhaul. Remainder of hulk maintained as a memorial at Pearl Harbor, HI.

Arizona BB-39 — Photograph taken, 19 June 1915, during her launching at the New York Navy Yard, Brooklyn, NY. When compared to the launch photograph of the USS Pennsylvania, Arizona's teak wood backing has not yet been fitted.

Arizona BB-39 — Photograph taken, 1921, while underway traversing the Panama Canal. (Official U.S. Navy Photo)

Arizona BB-39 — Photograph taken, March 1931, while underway at an unknown location with President Herbert Hoover on board in the Atlantic Ocean. Note the Presidential Flag flying from the mainmast peak. (Official U.S. Navy Photo)

Arizona BB-39 — Photograph taken, late April 1932, while underway at an unknown location off of the California coast pitching in heavy seas. (Official U.S. Navy Photo)

Arizona BB-39 — Photograph taken, circa 1935, while underway at an unknown location in the Pacific Ocean. (Official U.S. Navy Photo)

Arizona BB-39 — Photograph taken, circa late 1940, anchored off of Seattle, WA, just prior to her overhaul by the Puget Sound Navy Yard, Bremerton, WA. (Ray D. Bean photo collection)

Arizona BB-39 — Photograph taken, 7 December 1941, blowing up during the Japanese attack on Pearl Harbor, HI. (Official U.S. Navy Photo)

Arizona BB-39 — Photograph taken, 7 December 1941, blowing up during the Japanese attack on Pearl Harbor, HI. (Official U.S. Navy Photo)

Arizona BB-39 — Photograph taken, 7 December 1941, on fire from her forward magazines exploding during the Japanese attack on Pearl Harbor, HI (Official U.S. Navy Photo)

Arizona BB-39 — Photograph taken, 10 December 1941, sunk in the water as a result of damage received during the Japanese attack on Pearl Harbor, HI (Official U.S. Navy Photo)

<table>
<tr><th colspan="3">Class Specifications</th><th>As Completed (1916)</th><th>Operational Condition as of 1935</th></tr>
<tr><td rowspan="13">HULL</td><td rowspan="2">LENGTH</td><td>Waterline</td><td>600’ 0”</td><td>600’ 0”</td></tr>
<tr><td>Overall</td><td>608’ 0”</td><td>608’ 0”</td></tr>
<tr><td colspan="2">EXTREME BEAM</td><td>97’ .5”</td><td>106’ 3”</td></tr>
<tr><td rowspan="4">DISPLACEMENT</td><td rowspan="2">Full Load</td><td>32,567 tons</td><td>37,132 tons (BB-38)</td></tr>
<tr><td></td><td>37,654 tons (BB-39)</td></tr>
<tr><td rowspan="2">Normal</td><td>31,400 tons</td><td>33,100 tons (BB-38)</td></tr>
<tr><td></td><td>32,600 tons (BB-39)</td></tr>
<tr><td colspan="2">MAXIMUM DRAFT</td><td>29’ 10”</td><td>33’ 6”</td></tr>
<tr><td rowspan="5">COMPLEMENT</td><td rowspan="2">Officers</td><td>55</td><td>95 (BB-38)</td></tr>
<tr><td></td><td>93 (BB-39)</td></tr>
<tr><td rowspan="2">Enlisted</td><td>860</td><td>1,079 (BB-38)</td></tr>
<tr><td></td><td>959 (BB-39)</td></tr>
<tr><td>Marines</td><td>75</td><td>None</td></tr>
<tr><td rowspan="14">ARMAMENT</td><td rowspan="5"></td><td>Main</td><td>(4) triple 14”/45 B.L.R. turrets</td><td>(4) triple 14”/45 B.L.R. turrets</td></tr>
<tr><td rowspan="3">Secondary</td><td>(22) single 5”/51 mounts</td><td>(12) single 5”/51 mounts</td></tr>
<tr><td>(4) single 3”/50 AA mounts</td><td>(8) single 5”/25 AA mounts</td></tr>
<tr><td>(4) single 3 pdr.</td><td>(4) single 3 pdr. saluting</td></tr>
<tr><td>Torpedo Tubes</td><td>(2) 21” submerged</td><td>None</td></tr>
<tr><td rowspan="6">ARMOR</td><td>Belt</td><td>8” – 13.5”</td><td>8” – 13.5”</td></tr>
<tr><td>Bulkheads</td><td>8” – 13”</td><td>8” – 13”</td></tr>
<tr><td>Deck</td><td>3” – 6”</td><td>3” – 6”</td></tr>
<tr><td>Turrets</td><td>9” – 18”</td><td>9” – 18”</td></tr>
<tr><td>Barbettes</td><td>4.5” – 13”</td><td>4.5” – 13”</td></tr>
<tr><td>Conning Tower</td><td>16”</td><td>16”</td></tr>
<tr><td rowspan="3">AIRCRAFT</td><td>Number</td><td>None</td><td>3</td></tr>
<tr><td rowspan="2">Catapults</td><td rowspan="2">None</td><td>(1) top of #3 turret</td></tr>
<tr><td>(1) quarter deck aft</td></tr>
<tr><td rowspan="15">ENGINEERING</td><td rowspan="3">SPEED</td><td rowspan="2">Maximum</td><td>21.1 knots (BB-38)</td><td>20.9 knots (BB-38)</td></tr>
<tr><td>21.0 knots (BB-39)</td><td>20.1 knots (BB-39)</td></tr>
<tr><td>Economical</td><td>10.0 knots</td><td>10.0 knots</td></tr>
<tr><td rowspan="3">ENGINES</td><td rowspan="2">Manufacturer</td><td>Curtis (BB-38)</td><td>Curtis – Westinghouse (BB-38)</td></tr>
<tr><td>Parsons (BB-39)</td><td>Parsons – Westinghouse (BB-39)</td></tr>
<tr><td>Type</td><td>Geared Turbines</td><td>Geared Turbines</td></tr>
<tr><td rowspan="2">HORSEPOWER</td><td rowspan="2">Shaft</td><td>29,366 (BB-38)</td><td>33,376</td></tr>
<tr><td>34,000 (BB-39)</td><td></td></tr>
<tr><td colspan="2">SCREWS</td><td>4</td><td>4</td></tr>
<tr><td rowspan="4">BOILERS</td><td rowspan="2">Manufacturer</td><td>B & W</td><td>White-Forster & Bureau Express (BB-38)</td></tr>
<tr><td></td><td>Bureau Express (BB-39)</td></tr>
<tr><td rowspan="2">Type/No.</td><td>WT/12</td><td>WT/5 & 1 (BB-38)</td></tr>
<tr><td></td><td>WT/6 (BB-39)</td></tr>
<tr><td colspan="2">FUEL CAPACITY</td><td>2,322 tons oil</td><td>5,724 tons oil</td></tr>
<tr><td colspan="2">DRIVE</td><td>TRD</td><td>TRD</td></tr>
</table>

18: NEW MEXICO CLASS (BB-40 to BB-42)

New Mexico (BB-40)

NAME (HULL NO.)	BUILDER	KEEL LAID	LAUNCHED	COMMISSIONED
NEW MEXICO (BB-40)	New York NY	14 Oct 1915	23 Apr 1917	20 May 1918

Authorized 30 Jun 1914. Contract awarded 20 Oct 1914. Sponsored by Miss Margaret C. Debaca. First Commanding Officer: CAPT Ashley H. Robertson. Originally named CALIFORNIA. Renamed NEW MEXICO 22 Mar 1916. Rated as BATTLESHIP NO. 40. Classified BB-40 on 17 Jul 1920. Placed in reduced comm. 5 Mar 1931 for modernization at Philadelphia, PA. Rebuilt at Philadelphia Navy Yard (5 Mar 1931 – 22 Jan 1933). Placed in full comm. 22 Jan 1933. Decomm. 19 Jul 1946 at Boston, MA. Struck 25 Feb 1947 from the NVR. Sold 9 Nov 1947 to Lipsett Div., Liguria Bros., New York City, NY. Scrapped.

New Mexico BB-40 — Photograph taken, circa 1918–1919, anchored at an unknown location along the East Coast of the United States. (Official U.S. Navy Photo)

New Mexico BB-40 — Photograph taken, mid 1930s, while underway at an unknown location in the Pacific Ocean following an extensive rebuilding by the Philadelphia Navy Yard, Philadelphia, PA.

New Mexico BB-40 — Photograph taken, 31 December 1941, tied up to a pier, looking forward from the stern during an overhaul by the Norfolk Navy Yard, Portsmouth, VA. Note that she was painted out in a Measure 12 Modified camouflage pattern. (Official U.S. Navy Photo)

New Mexico BB-40 — Photograph taken, 31 December 1941, tied up to a pier during an overhaul by the Norfolk Navy Yard, Portsmouth, VA. Note that she was painted out in a Measure 12 Modified camouflage pattern and the numerous light AA guns that had been added amidships. (Official U.S. Navy Photo)

New Mexico BB-40 — Photograph taken, 31 December 1941, tied up to a pier during an overhaul by the Norfolk Navy Yard, Portsmouth, VA. Note that she was painted out in a Measure 12 Modified camouflage pattern and her hull number painted on top of number two turret. (Official U.S. Navy Photo)

New Mexico BB-40 — Photograph taken, 6 October 1943, anchored in Sinclair Inlet, WA, following an overhaul by the Puget Sound Navy Yard, Bremerton, WA. Note that she wore a Measure 21 camouflage pattern. (Official U.S. Navy Photo)

New Mexico BB-40 — Photograph taken, 31 January 1944, while underway off of Kwajalein Atoll, Marshall Islands in the Pacific Ocean. Note that turret number one was trained out to starboard. (Ray D. Bean photo collection)

New Mexico BB-40 — Photograph taken, 16 June 1944, while underway off of Guam during the first bombardment of the island in the Pacific Ocean. Note that number one, two and four turrets were trained to starboard and the low-flying aircraft over the coast. (Official U.S. Navy Photo)

New Mexico BB-40 — Photographs taken, 21 October 1944, while underway in Sinclair Inlet, WA, following an overhaul by the Puget Sound Navy Yard, Bremerton, WA. Note that she wore a Measure 32/6D camouflage pattern. (Official U.S. Navy Photo)

NAME (HULL NO.)	BUILDER	KEEL LAID	LAUNCHED	COMMISSIONED
MISSISSIPPI (BB-41)	NNS&DD Co.	5 Apr 1915	25 Jan 1917	18 Dec 1917

Authorized 30 Jun 1914. Contract awarded 23 Nov 1914. Sponsored by Miss Camille McBeath. First Commanding Officer: CAPT Joseph L. Jayne. Rated as BATTLESHIP NO. 41. Classified BB-41 on 17 Jul 1920. Placed in reduced comm. 30 Jan 1931 for modernization at Norfolk, VA. Rebuilt at Norfolk Navy Yard (30 Jan 1931–31 Aug 1932). Placed in full comm. 31 Aug 1932. Reclass. AG-128 on 15 Feb 1946. Rebuilt as test and experimental ship at Norfolk Naval Shipyard (November 1945–July 1947). Decomm. 17 Sep 1956 at Norfolk, VA. Struck 30 Jul 1956 from the NVR. Sold 28 Nov 1956 to the Bethlehem Steel Co., Bethlehem, PA, for $1,660.764.00. Scrapped.

Mississippi BB-41 — Photograph taken, circa 1917–1918, anchored at an unknown location along the East Coast of the United States. (Official U.S. Navy Photo)

Mississippi BB-41 — Photograph taken, 31 May 1934, while underway at an unknown location during a fleet review along the East Coast of the United States. Note the ship's crew manning the rails in their blue uniforms. (Official U.S. Navy Photo)

Mississippi BB-41 — Photograph taken, 13 July 1944, while underway making three knots in Puget Sound, WA, during an overhaul by the Puget Sound Navy Yard, Bremerton, WA. Note that she wore a Measure 32/6D camouflage pattern. (Official U.S. Navy Photo)

Mississippi BB-41 — Photograph taken, 16 July 1944, while underway, in overcast weather, in Sinclair Inlet, WA, during an overhaul by the Puget Sound Navy Yard, Bremerton, WA. Note that she wore a Measure 32/6D camouflage pattern. (Official U.S. Navy Photo)

Mississippi BB-41 — Photograph taken, 21 July 1944, while underway in Puget Sound, WA, practicing a different type of refueling with USS Thorn (DD-647). A hose was trailed behind the refueling ship and was picked up by receiving ship. The receiving ship would then hookup the hose and refueling would begin. Note that she wore a Measure 32/6D camouflage pattern. (Official U.S. Navy Photo)

Mississippi BB-41 — Photograph taken, 12 September 1944, while underway supporting the invasion of Peleliu Island, Palau Islands, in the Pacific Ocean. Note that she wore a Measure 32/6D camouflage pattern. (Official U.S. Navy Photo)

Mississippi AG-128 — Photograph taken, circa 1947–1948, anchored at an unknown location along the East Coast of the United States. Note that she still retained her number four turret and the aft catapult. (Official U.S. Navy Photo)

Mississippi AG-128 — Photograph taken, circa mid 1950's, while underway at an unknown location in the Atlantic Ocean. Note the 6"/47 turret in place of number one 14" turret forward, the twin 5"/38 gun mounts amidships, the two twin Terrier guided missile launchers aft, and the movie screen set up on the fantail. (Official U.S. Navy Photo)

Mississippi AG-128 — Photograph taken, February 1955, while underway at an unknown location in the Atlantic Ocean. Note the 6"/47 turret in place of number one 14" turret forward, the twin 5"/38 gun mounts amidships, the two twin Terrier guided missile launchers aft, and the movie screen set up on the fantail. (Official U.S. Navy Photo)

Mississippi AG-128 — Photograph taken, circa mid 1950's, while underway at an unknown location in the Atlantic Ocean. Note the 6"/47 turret in place of number one 14" turret forward, the two single 5"/38 gun mounts amidships, and the two twin Terrier guided missile launchers aft. (Official U.S. Navy Photo)

NAME (HULL NO.)	BUILDER	KEEL LAID	LAUNCHED	COMMISSIONED
IDAHO (BB-42)	NY Ship Corp.	20 Jan 1915	30 Jun 1917	24 Mar 1919

Authorized 30 Jun 1914. Contract awarded 9 Nov 1914. Sponsored by Miss Henrietta A. Limons. First Commanding Officer: CAPT Carl T. Vogelgesang. Rated as BATTLESHIP NO. 42. Classified BB-42 on 17 Jul 1920. Placed in reduced comm. 30 Sep 1933 for modernization at Norfolk, VA. Rebuilt at Norfolk Navy Yard (30 Sep 1933 – 9 Oct 1934). Placed in full comm. 9 Oct 1934. Rebuilt again at Puget Sound Navy Yard (22 Oct 1944 – 1 Jan 1945). Decomm. 3 Jul 1946 at Norfolk, VA. Struck 16 Sep 1947 from the NVR. Sold 24 Nov 1947 to Lipsett Div., Liguria Bros., New York City, NY. Scrapped.

Idaho BB-42 — Photograph taken, circa 1919, while underway at high speed at an unknown location along the East Coast of the United States. Note the signalmen atop number two turret using semaphore flags. (Official U.S. Navy Photo)

Idaho BB-42 — Photograph taken, August 1919, while going through the Gatun Locks of the Panama Canal. Note the seaplane on the catapult on the fantail and the ship's name on the stern. (Ray D. Bean photo collection)

Idaho BB-42 — Photograph taken, 25 February 1935, while underway in Boston Harbor, Boston MA, following a repair availability by the Boston Navy Yard, Boston, MA. Note the ship's name on the stern.

Idaho BB-42 — Photograph taken, 24 December 1942, anchored in Sinclair Inlet, WA, following an overhaul by the Puget Sound Navy Yard, Bremerton, WA. Note that she wore a Measure 21 camouflage pattern. (Official U.S. Navy Photo)

Idaho BB-42 — Photograph taken, 15 August 1944, while entering floating drydock USS ABSD-1 at Espiritu Santo, Vanuatu, for repairs to her "blisters." Note that she wore a Measure 21 camouflage pattern and the hundreds of sailors on her decks. (Official U.S. Navy Photo)

Idaho BB-42 — Photograph taken, 15 August 1944, in floating drydock USS ABSD-1 at Espiritu Santo, Vanuatu, for repairs to her "blisters." Note all of the support craft alongside the floating drydock. (Official U.S. Navy Photo)

Idaho BB-42 — Photograph taken, 7 January 1945, while underway making 12 knots in Puget Sound, WA, following an overhaul by the Puget Sound Navy Yard, Bremerton, WA. Note that she wore a Measure 21 camouflage pattern and the five single 5"/38 gun mounts amidships that were added during the overhaul. (Official U.S. Navy Photo)

Idaho BB-42 — Photograph taken, 19 February 1945, while underway during the bombardment of Iwo Jima. Note all of her gun turrets are trained on the island. (Official U.S. Navy Photo)

Idaho BB-42 — Photograph taken, circa 1946–1947 tied up to a pier at Norfolk, VA. Note that she has been decommissioned and the large white building that are covering her turrets. (Official U.S. Navy Photo)

Class Specifications			As Completed (1917/1919)	Operational Condition as of 1938
HULL	LENGTH	Waterline	600’ 0”	600’ 0”
		Overall	624’ 0”	624’ 0”
	EXTREME BEAM		97’ 4.5”	106’ 3”
	DISPLACEMENT	Full Load	33,000 tons	36,000 tons
		Standard		33,400 tons (BB-40, 42)
				33,000 tons (BB-41)
		Normal	32,000 tons	
	MAXIMUM DRAFT		31’ 0.5”	34’ 0”
	COMPLEMENT	Officers	70 (BB-40), 67 (BB-41)	102 (BB-40)
			68 (BB-42)	90 (BB-41, 42)
		Enlisted	1,251 (BB-40)	1,156 (BB-40)
			1,176 (BB-41)	1,353 (BB-41)
			1,167 (BB-42)	1,413 (BB-42)
		Marines	60 (BB-40), 67 (BB-41)	None
			34 (BB-42)	
ARMAMENT		Main	(4) triple 14”/50 turrets	(4) triple 14”/50 turrets
		Secondary	(22) single 5”/51 mounts (BB-40, 41)	(12) single 5”/51 mounts
			(14) single 5”/51 mounts (BB-42)	(8) single 5”/25 AA mounts
			(4) single 3”/50 AA mounts	(2) single 6 pdr. saluting BB-40, 41)
			(4) single 6 pdr. saluting (BB-40, 41)	(2) single 3 pdr. saluting (BB-42)
			(4) single 3 pdr. saluting (BB-42)	
		Torpedo Tubes	(2) 21” submerged	None
	ARMOR	Belt	8” – 13.5”	8” – 13.5”
		Bulkheads	8” – 13.5”	8” – 13.5”
		Deck	4” – 6”	4” – 6”
		Turrets	9” – 18”	9” – 18”
		Barbettes	4.5” – 13”	4.5” – 13”
		Conning Tower	16”	16”
	AIRCRAFT	Number	None	3
		Catapults	None	(1) top of #3 turret
				(1) quarter deck aft
ENGINEERING	SPEED	Maximum	21.1 knots	22.0 knots
		Economical	10.0 knots	10.0 knots
	ENGINES	Manufacturer	General Electric (BB-40)	Westinghouse
			Curtis (BB-41)	
			Parsons (BB-42)	
		Type	Turbo-Electric (BB-40)	Geared Turbines
			Geared Turbines (BB-41, 42)	
	HORSEPOWER	Shaft	31,197 (BB-40)	40,000
			31,804 (BB-41)	
			33,100 (BB-42)	
	SCREWS		4	4
	BOILERS	Manufacturer	B & W	White-Forster (BB-40)
				Bureau Express (BB-41, 42)
		Type/No.	WT/9	WT/4 (BB-40)
				WT/6 (BB-41, 42)
	FUEL CAPACITY		3,277 tons oil	5,401 tons oil
	DRIVE		TED (BB-40)	TRD
			TRD (BB-41, 42)	

19: TENNESSEE CLASS (BB-43 to BB-44)

Tennessee (BB-43)

NAME (HULL NO.)	BUILDER	KEEL LAID	LAUNCHED	COMMISSIONED
TENNESSEE (BB-43)	New York NY	14 May 1917	30 Apr 1919	3 Jun 1920

Authorized 3 Mar 1915. Contract awarded 28 Dec 1915. Sponsored by Miss Helen L. Roberts. First Commanding Officer: CAPT Richard H. Leigh. Rated as BATTLESHIP NO. 43. Classified BB-43 on 17 Jul 1920. Rebuilt at Puget Sound Navy Yard (September 1942 – May 1943). Decomm. 14 Feb 1947 at Philadelphia, PA. Struck 1 Mar 1959 from the NVR. Sold 16 Jul 1959 to the Bethlehem Steel Co., Bethlehem, PA, for $724,999.00. Scrapped.

Tennessee BB-43 — Photograph taken, February 1942, after her first post-Pearl Harbor modifications were completed by Puget Sound Navy Yard, Bremerton, WA. (Ray D. Bean photo collection)

Tennessee BB-43 — Photograph taken, 26 February 1942, anchored in Sinclair Inlet, WA, following a major refit by the Puget Sound Navy Yard, Bremerton, WA. Note that she wore a Measure 21 camouflage pattern and the barrage balloons over the Navy Yard. Also note that the aft superstructure has been cut down. (Official U.S. Navy Photo)

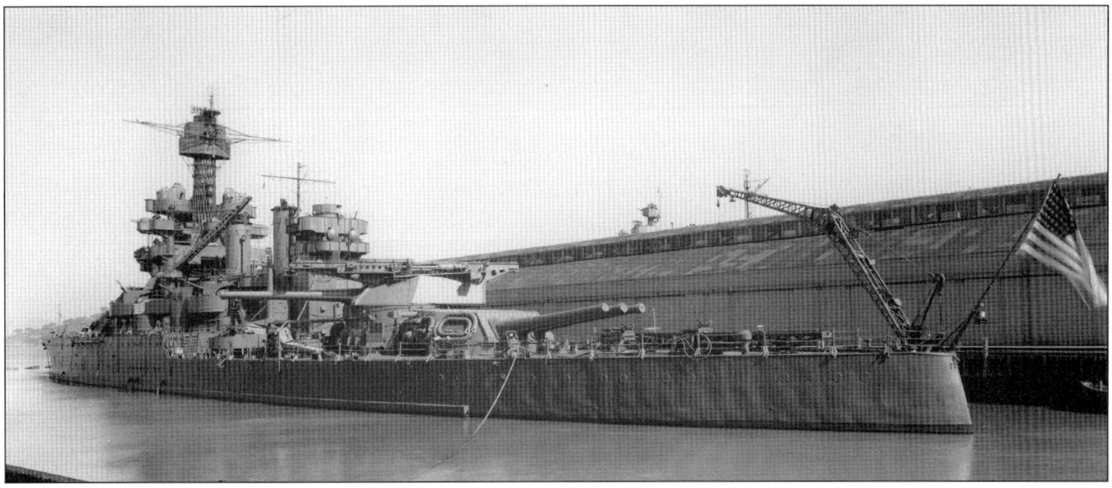

Tennessee BB-43 — Photograph taken, 15 March 1942, tied up to a pier in North San Francisco, CA. Note that she wore a Measure 21 camouflage pattern and the new shields on the AA guns amidships. Also note that the aft superstructure had been cut down and the stern port holes have been plated over. (Official U.S. Navy Photo)

Tennessee BB-43 — Photograph taken, 8 May 1943, while underway in Sinclair Inlet, WA, following a complete rebuilding by the Puget Sound Navy Yard, Bremerton, WA. Note that she wore a Measure 14 camouflage pattern. (Official U.S. Navy Photo)

Tennessee BB-43 — Photograph taken, 12 May 1943, while underway at high speed on sea trials off of Port Angeles, WA, after having been completely rebuilt by the Puget Sound Navy Yard, Bremerton, WA. Note that she wore a Measure 14 camouflage pattern. (Official U.S. Navy Photo)

Tennessee BB-43 — Photograph taken, 12 May 1943, while underway at high speed on sea trials off of Port Angeles, WA, after having been completely rebuilt by the Puget Sound Navy Yard, Bremerton, WA. Note that she wore a Measure 14 camouflage pattern and that number four turret was trained to starboard. (Official U.S. Navy Photo)

Tennessee BB-43 — Photograph taken, 12 May 1943, while underway at high speed on sea trials off of Port Angeles, WA, after having been completely rebuilt by the Puget Sound Navy Yard, Bremerton, WA. Note that she wore a Measure 14 camouflage pattern. (Official U.S. Navy Photo)

Tennessee BB-43 — Photographs taken, 11 January 1944, anchored in San Pedro Harbor, San Pedro, CA. Note that she wore a Measure 32/1D camouflage pattern and the crew's bedding being aired out. (Official U.S. Navy Photo)

Tennessee BB-43 — Photograph taken, 25 January 1945, while underway in Sinclair Inlet, WA, following an overhaul by the Puget Sound Naval Shipyard, Bremerton, WA. Note that she wore a Measure 21 camouflage pattern. (Official U.S. Navy Photo)

California (BB-44)

NAME (HULL NO.)	BUILDER	KEEL LAID	LAUNCHED	COMMISSIONED
CALIFORNIA (BB-44)	Mare I.	25 Oct 1916	20 Nov 1919	10 Aug 1921

Authorized 3 Mar 1915. Contract awarded 5 Jan 1916. Sponsored by Mrs. Barbara S. Zane. First Commanding Officer: CAPT Henry J. Ziegemeier. Rated as BATTLESHIP NO. 44. Classified BB-44 on 17 Jul 1920. Rebuilt at Puget Sound Navy Yard (7 Jun 1942 – 31 Jan 1944). Decomm. 14 Feb 1947 at Philadelphia, PA. Struck 1 Mar 1959 from the NVR. Sold 1 Jul 1959 to the Bethlehem Steel Co., Bethlehem, PA, for $859,999.00. Scrapped.

California BB-44 — Photograph taken, circa 1921, while underway at high speed at an unknown location during builder's sea trials along the West Coast of the United States. (Official U.S. Navy Photo)

California BB-44 — Photograph taken, September 1921, while underway in San Francisco Bay, CA, for sea trials.

California BB-44 — Photograph taken, 7 December 1941, listing to port after taking a number of torpedo hits during the Japanese attack on Pearl Harbor, HI. (Official U.S. Navy Photo)

California BB-44 — Photograph taken, 10 October 1942, while underway in Pearl Harbor, HI, heading for the Puget Sound Navy Yard, Bremerton, WA, for a complete rebuilding. (Official U.S. Navy Photo)

California BB-44 — Photograph taken, 18 January 1944, anchored in Sinclair Inlet, WA, during a complete rebuilding by the Puget Sound Navy Yard, Bremerton, WA. Note that she wore a Measure 32/16D camouflage pattern. (Official U.S. Navy Photo)

California BB-44 — Photograph taken, 25 January 1944, while underway making eight knots in the Straits of Juan de Fuca, WA, following a complete rebuilding by the Puget Sound Navy Yard, Bremerton, WA. Note that she wore a Measure 32/16D camouflage pattern. (Official U.S. Navy Photo)

California BB-44 — Photograph taken, 8 September 1944, in floating drydock USS ABSD-1 at Espiritu Santo, Vanuatu, for collision damage repairs. On 23 August 1944, she was hit by USS Tennessee (BB-43) due to a steering casualty. The collision left a large gash forward of number one turret. Note all of the support craft alongside the floating drydock. (Official U.S. Navy Photo)

California BB-44 — Photographs taken, 25 April 1945, while underway making 20 knots on sea trials in Puget Sound, WA, during an overhaul by the Puget Sound Naval Shipyard, Bremerton, WA. Note that she wore a Measure 21 camouflage pattern and her very wide beam. (Official U.S. Navy Photo)

California BB-44 — Photograph taken, 28 April 1945, anchored in Sinclair Inlet, WA, during an overhaul by the Puget Sound Naval Shipyard, Bremerton, WA. Note that she wore a Measure 21 camouflage pattern and that the Union Jack and National Ensign are at half-staff for the recent death of President Franklin D. Roosevelt. (Official U.S. Navy Photo)

Class Specifications			As Completed (1920/1921)	Operational Condition as of 1945
HULL	LENGTH	Waterline	600' 0"	600' 0"
		Overall	624' 0"	624' 0" (BB-43)
				625' 0" (BB-44)
	EXTREME BEAM		97' 3.75"	114' 0"
	DISPLACEMENT	Full Load	33,190 tons	40,354 tons
		Standard	32,300 tons	32,300 tons (BB-43)
				32,600 tons (BB-44)
	MAXIMUM DRAFT		31' 0"	34' 0"
	COMPLEMENT	Officers	67 (BB-43)	114 (BB-43)
			66 (BB-44)	141 (BB-44)
		Enlisted	1,328	2,129 (BB-43)
				2,234 (BB-44)
		Marines	75	None
ARMAMENT		Main	(4) triple 14"/50 turrets	(4) triple 14"/50 turrets
		Secondary	(14) single 5"/51 mounts	(8) twin 5"/38 DP. mounts
			(4) single 3"/50 AA mounts	(10) quad 40-mm mounts (BB-43)
			(4) single 6 pdr. saluting	(43) single 20-mm mounts (BB-43)
				(40) twin 20-mm mounts (BB-44)
		Torpedo Tubes	(2) 21" submerged	None
	ARMOR	Belt	8" – 13.5"	8" – 13.5"
		Bulkheads	13.5"	13.5"
		Deck	2.5" – 3.5"	2.5" – 3.5"
		Turrets	9" – 18"	9" – 18"
		Barbettes	13"	13"
		5" Gun Mounts	None	1" – 1.5"
		5" Gun Barbettes	None	1.5"
		Conning Tower	16"	16"
	AIRCRAFT	Number	None	3
		Catapults	None	(1) quarter deck aft
ENGINEERING	SPEED	Maximum	21.4 knots (BB-43)	20.8 knots (BB-43)
			21.5 knots (BB-44)	19.8 knots (BB-44)
		Economical	10.0 knots	10.0 knots
	ENGINES	Manufacturer	Westinghouse (BB-43)	Westinghouse (BB-43)
			General Electric (BB-44)	General Electric (BB-44)
		Type	Turbo-Electric	Turbo-Electric
	HORSEPOWER	Shaft	26,800 (BB-43)	30,000 (BB-43)
			28,500 (BB-44)	29,500 (BB-44)
	SCREWS		4	4
	BOILERS	Manufacturer	B & W (BB-43)	B & W (BB-43)
			Bureau Express (BB-44)	Bureau Express (BB-44)
		Type/No.	WT/8	WT/8
	FUEL CAPACITY		4,656 tons oil	31,123 barrels oil (BB-43)
				30,801 barrels oil (BB-44)
				434 barrels diesel oil (BB-43)
				417 barrels diesel oil (BB-44)
				4,015 gallons gasoline (BB-43)
				4,301 gallons gasoline (BB-44)
	DRIVE		TED	TED

Colorado (BB-45)

NAME (HULL NO.)	BUILDER	KEEL LAID	LAUNCHED	COMMISSIONED
COLORADO (BB-45)	NY Ship Corp.	29 May 1919	22 Mar 1921	30 Aug 1923

Authorized 29 Aug 1916. Contract awarded 17 Jan 1917. Sponsored by Mrs. Ruth N. Melville. First Commanding Officer: CAPT Reginald R. Belknap. Rated as BATTLESHIP NO. 45. Classified BB-45 on 17 Jul 1920. Decomm. 7 Jan 1947 at Bremerton, WA. Struck 1 Mar 1959 from the NVR. Sold 6 Jul 1959 to The Learner Co., Oakland, CA, for $611,777.77. Scrapped.

Colorado BB-45 — Photograph taken, 1923, while underway at high speed at an unknown location probably during builder's sea trials along the East Coast of the United States. (Official U.S. Navy Photo)

Colorado BB-45 — Photograph taken, 25 April 1944, while underway in Sinclair Inlet, WA, during an overhaul by the Puget Sound Navy Yard, Bremerton, WA. Note the camouflage pattern that she wore. (Official U.S. Navy Photo)

Colorado BB-45 — Photograph taken, 26 April 1944, while underway making 15 knots off of Point Madison, WA, during an overhaul by the Puget Sound Navy Yard, Bremerton, WA. Note the camouflage pattern that she wore. (Official U.S. Navy Photo)

Colorado BB-45 — Photograph taken, 27 July 1944, anchored off of Tinian Island, Northern Mariana Islands, showing her battle damage. On 24 July 1944, she was hit by 6" shells from a Japanese shore battery on Tinian Island. Note the camouflage pattern that she wore. (Official U.S. Navy Photo)

Colorado BB-45 — Photograph taken, 2 October 1944, while underway in Sinclair Inlet, WA, on sea trials during a refit by the Puget Sound Navy Yard, Bremerton, WA. Note the camouflage pattern that she wore. (Official U.S. Navy Photo)

Colorado BB-45 — Photograph taken, 2 October 1944, while underway in Sinclair Inlet, WA, on sea trials during a refit by the Puget Sound Navy Yard, Bremerton, WA. Note the camouflage pattern that she wore. (Official U.S. Navy Photo)

Colorado BB-45 — Photograph taken, 3 October 1944, while underway making 19.2 knots on sea trials in Puget Sound, WA, during a refit by the Puget Sound Naval Shipyard, Bremerton, WA. Note her very wide beam. (Official U.S. Navy Photo)

Colorado BB-45 — Photograph taken, 3 October 1944, while underway making 19.2 knots on sea trials in Puget Sound, WA, during a refit by the Puget Sound Naval Shipyard, Bremerton, WA. Note the camouflage pattern that she wore. (Official U.S. Navy Photo)

Colorado BB-45 — Photograph taken, 3 October 1944, while underway making 19.2 knots on sea trials in Puget Sound, WA, during a refit by the Puget Sound Naval Shipyard, Bremerton, WA. Note the camouflage pattern that she wore. (Official U.S. Navy Photo)

Colorado BB-45 — Photograph taken, 15 October 1945, as the ship arrived in San Francisco, CA, following the end of World War II. The ship's crew, in their dress blues, manned the rails and what appeared to be a long "homeward bound" pennant streaming from the stern aircraft crane. Note that she wore a Measure 21 camouflage pattern. (Ray D. Bean photo collection)

NAME (HULL NO.)	BUILDER	KEEL LAID	LAUNCHED	COMMISSIONED
MARYLAND (BB-46)	NNS&DD Co.	24 Apr 1917	20 Mar 1920	21 Jul 1921

Authorized 29 Aug 1916. Contract awarded 5 Dec 1916. Sponsored by Mrs. E. Brooke Lee. First Commanding Officer: CAPT Charles F. Preston. Rated as BATTLESHIP NO. 46. Classified BB-46 on 17 Jul 1920. Decomm. 30 Apr 1947 at Bremerton, WA. Struck 1 Mar 1959 from the NVR. Sold 15 Jul 1959 to The Learner Co., Oakland, CA, for $676,777.77. Scrapped.

Maryland BB-46 — Photograph taken, 23 August 1935, while underway at an unknown location in the Pacific Ocean.

Maryland BB-46 — Photograph taken, 7 December 1941, tied up to a quay during the Japanese attack on Pearl Harbor, HI. Note the battleship next to her, USS Oklahoma (BB-37), had already rolled over. (Official U.S. Navy Photo)

Maryland BB-46 — Photograph taken, 9 February 1942, while underway in Sinclair Inlet, WA, during a repair availability by the Puget Sound Navy Yard, Bremerton, WA. Note that she wore a Measure 21 camouflage pattern and the new shields on the AA guns amidships. (Official U.S. Navy Photo)

Maryland BB-46 — Photographs taken, 25 April 1944, while underway in Sinclair Inlet, WA, following an overhaul by the Puget Sound Navy Yard, Bremerton, WA. Note the camouflage pattern that she wore and the new shields on the AA guns amidships. (Official U.S. Navy Photo)

Maryland BB-46 — Photograph taken, 26 April 1944, while underway making 20 knots on sea trials off of Pillar Point, WA, following an overhaul by the Puget Sound Navy Yard, Bremerton, WA. Note the camouflage pattern that she wore. (Official U.S. Navy Photo)

Maryland BB-46 — Photograph taken, 1 May 1944, while underway at high speed running post-overhaul speed trials in Puget Sound, WA, following an overhaul by the Puget Sound Navy Yard, Bremerton, WA. Note the camouflage pattern that she wore. (Official U.S. Navy Photo)

Maryland BB-46 — Photographs taken, 5 August 1945, while underway in Sinclair Inlet, WA, during an overhaul by the Puget Sound Naval Shipyard, Bremerton, WA. Note that she wore a Measure 21 camouflage pattern. (Official U.S. Navy Photo)

Maryland BB-46 — Photograph taken, 5 August 1945, while underway making 16 knots on sea trials in Puget Sound, WA, during an overhaul by the Puget Sound Naval Shipyard, Bremerton, WA. Note that she wore a Measure 21 camouflage pattern and her very wide beam. (Official U.S. Navy Photo)

Washington (BB-47)

NAME (HULL NO.)	BUILDER	KEEL LAID	LAUNCHED	COMMISSIONED
WASHINGTON (BB-47)	NY Ship Corp.	30 Jun 1919	1 Sep 1921	NEVER

Authorized 29 Aug 1916. Contract awarded 17 Jan 1917. Sponsored by Miss Jean Summers. Rated as BATTLESHIP NO. 47. Classified BB-47 on 17 Jul 1920. Construction suspended 8 Feb 1922 when 75.9% completed and cancelled 17 Aug 1923 in accordance with the terms of the Washington Treaty for Naval Limitations. Struck 10 Nov 1923 from the NVR. Hull used as a target in weapons tests. Sunk 25 Nov 1924 by naval gunfire, bombs and torpedoes off the Virginia Capes.

Washington BB-47 — Photograph taken, 5 April 1922, tied up to a pier at the New York Shipbuilding Corp., Camden, NJ. Her construction had been suspended two months earlier, under the terms of the Washington Naval Limitations treaty.

West Virginia (BB-48)

NAME (HULL NO.)	BUILDER	KEEL LAID	LAUNCHED	COMMISSIONED
WEST VIRGINIA (BB-48)	NNS&DD Co.	12 Apr 1920	19 Nov 1921	1 Dec 1923

Authorized 29 Aug 1916. Contract awarded 5 Dec 1916. Sponsored by Miss Alice W. Mann. First Commanding Officer: CAPT Thomas J. Senn. Rated as BATTLESHIP NO. 48. Classified BB-48 on 17 Jul 1920. Rebuilt at Puget Sound Navy Yard (1942 – September 1944). Decomm. 9 Jan 1947 at Bremerton, WA. Struck 1 Mar 1959 from the NVR. Sold 24 Aug 1959 to the Union Minerals & Alloys Corp., New York City, NY, for $781,298.89. Scrapped.

West Virginia BB-48 — Photograph taken, December 1923, while underway in Hampton Roads, VA, shortly after commissioning. (Official U.S. Navy Photo)

West Virginia BB-48 — Photograph taken, 7 December 1941, as she settled into the harbor bottom on an even keel during the Japanese attack on Pearl Harbor, HI. (Official U.S. Navy Photo)

West Virginia BB-48 — Photograph taken, May 1943, while underway off of Pearl Harbor, HI, heading for the Puget Sound Navy Yard, Bremerton, WA, for a complete rebuilding.

West Virginia BB-48 — Photographs taken, 2 July 1944, while underway in Sinclair Inlet, WA, during a complete rebuilding by the Puget Sound Navy Yard, Bremerton, WA. Note that she wore a Measure 32/7D camouflage pattern. (Official U.S. Navy Photo)

West Virginia BB-48 — Photograph taken, 2 July 1944, while underway in Sinclair Inlet, WA, during a complete rebuilding by the Puget Sound Navy Yard, Bremerton, WA. Note that she wore a Measure 32/7D camouflage pattern. (Official U.S. Navy Photo)

West Virginia BB-48 — Photograph taken, 11 July 1944, while underway making three knots on sea trials in Puget Sound, WA, during a complete rebuilding by the Puget Sound Navy Yard, Bremerton, WA. Note that she wore a Measure 32/7D camouflage pattern. (Official U.S. Navy Photo)

West Virginia BB-48 — Photograph taken, 9 November 1944, in floating drydock USS ABSD-1 at Espiritu Santo, Vanuatu, to repair her damaged screws. On 21 October 1944, she touched bottom, slightly damaging three of her four screws. Note all of the support craft alongside the floating drydock. (Official U.S. Navy Photo)

West Virginia BB-48 — Photograph taken, circa late 1945, anchored in San Francisco Bay CA, completing a "Magic Carpet" run between Pearl Harbor, HI, and San Francisco, CA. Note that she wore a Measure 21 camouflage pattern. (Official U.S. Navy Photo)

Class Specifications			As Completed (1921/1923)	Operational Condition as of 1945
HULL	LENGTH	Waterline	600' 0"	600' 0"
		Overall	624' 0"	624' 6" (BB-45, 46)
				624' 0" (BB-48)
	EXTREME BEAM		97' 3.5"	108' 1" (BB-45, 46)
				114' 0" (BB-48)
	DISPLACEMENT	Full Load	33,590 tons	40,396 tons (BB-45)
				39,100 tons (BB-46)
				40,354 tons (BB-48)
		Standard	32,500 tons (BB-45)	32,500 tons (BB-45)
			31,500 tons (BB-46)	31,500 tons (BB-46)
			31,800 tons (BB-48)	31,800 tons (BB-48)
	MAXIMUM DRAFT		35' 6"	34' 9" (BB-45)
				33' 7" (BB-46)
				34' 0" (BB-48)
	COMPLEMENT	Officers	64	120 (BB-45)
				135 (BB-46)
				131 (BB-48)
		Enlisted	1,241	1,848 (BB-45)
				1,914 (BB-46)
				2,051 (BB-48)
		Marines	75	None
ARMAMENT		Main	(4) twin 16"/45 turrets	(4) twin 16"/45 turrets
		Secondary	(14) single 5"/51 mounts (BB-46)	(8) single 5"/38 DP mounts (BB-45)
			(12) single 5"/51 mounts (BB-45, 48)	(8) twin 5"/38 DP mounts (BB-46, 48)
			(8) single 3"/50 AA mounts (BB-45, 48)	(8) single 5"/25 DP mounts (BB-45)
			(4) single 3"/50 AA mounts (BB-46)	(12) quad 40-mm mounts (BB-46)
			(4) single 6 pdr. saluting	(10) quad 40-mm mounts (BB-45, 48)
				(1) quad 20-mm mounts (BB-48)
				(1) twin 20-mm mounts (BB-48)
				(44) single 20-mm mounts (BB-45)
				(35) single 20-mm mounts (BB-46)
				(58) single 20-mm mounts (BB-48)
		Torpedo Tubes	(2) 21" submerged	None
	ARMOR	Belt	8" – 13.5"	8" – 16"
		Bulkheads	13.5"	13.5"
		Deck	2.5" – 3.5"	2.5" – 3.5"
		Turrets	9" – 18"	9" – 18"
		Barbettes	4.5" – 13"	4.5" – 13"
		5" Gun Mounts	None	1" – 1.5"
		5" Gun Barbettes	None	1.5"
		Conning Tower	16"	16"
	AIRCRAFT	Number	None	3
		Catapults	None	(1) quarter deck aft
ENGINEERING	SPEED	Maximum	20.7 knots (BB-45)	21.7 knots (BB-45)
			21.1 knots (BB-46, 48)	21.6 knots (BB-46)
				21.1 knots (BB-48)
		Economical	10.0 knots	10.0 knots
	ENGINES	Manufacturer	Westinghouse (BB-45)	Westinghouse (BB-45)
			General Electric (BB-46, 48)	General Electric (BB-46, 48)
		Type	Turbo-Electric	Turbo-Electric
	HORSEPOWER	Shaft	28,900 (BB-45, 48)	32,000 (BB-45)
			36,167 (BB-46)	29,500 (BB-46, 48)
	SCREWS		4	4
	BOILERS	Manufacturer	B & W	B & W
		Type/No.	WT/8	WT/8
	FUEL CAPACITY		4,656 tons oil (BB-45)	34,640 barrels oil (BB-45)
			4,794 tons oil (BB-46, 48)	34,646 barrels oil (BB-46)
				30,976 barrels oil (BB-48)
				179 barrels diesel oil (BB-45)
				396 barrels diesel oil (BB-46)
				429 barrels diesel oil (BB-48)
				3,220 gallons gasoline (BB-45)
				4,785 gallons gasoline (BB-46)
				4,301 gallons gasoline (BB-48)
	DRIVE		TED	TED

21: SOUTH DAKOTA CLASS (BB-49 to BB-54)

South Dakota (BB-49)

NAME (HULL NO.)	BUILDER	KEEL LAID	LAUNCHED	COMMISSIONED
SOUTH DAKOTA (BB-49)	New York NY	15 Mar 1920	NEVER	NEVER

Authorized 4 Mar 1917. Contract awarded 2 Jul 1918. Rated as BATTLESHIP NO. 49. Classified BB-49 on 17 Jul 1920. Construction suspended 8 Feb 1922 when 38.5% completed and cancelled 17 Aug 1923 in accordance with the terms of the Washington Treaty for Naval Limitations. Struck 24 Aug 1923 from the NVR. Hull sold 25 Oct 1923 to the Steel Scrap Co., Philadelphia, PA. Scrapped on the ways.

South Dakota Class BB-49/54 — A 1922 artist's rendering of this class of ship underway. Painting by Rose Stokes.

South Dakota BB-49 — Photograph taken, 10 March 1922, looking forward from the stern, while under construction by the New York Navy Yard, Brooklyn, NY. Note the canvas covered barbettes. (Official U.S. Navy Photo)

NAME (HULL NO.)	BUILDER	KEEL LAID	LAUNCHED	COMMISSIONED
INDIANA (BB-50)	New York NY	1 Nov 1920	NEVER	NEVER

Authorized 4 Mar 1917. Contract awarded 2 Jul 1918. Rated as BATTLESHIP NO. 50. Classified BB-50 on 17 Jul 1920. Construction suspended 8 Feb 1922 when 34.7% completed and cancelled 17 Aug 1923 in accordance with the terms of the Washington Treaty for Naval Limitations. Struck 24 Aug 1923 from the NVR. Sold 25 Oct 1923 to the Steel Scrap Co., Philadelphia, PA. Scrapped on the ways.

Indiana BB-50 — Photograph taken, 10 March 1922, looking forward from the stern, while under construction by the New York Navy Yard, Brooklyn, NY. (Official U.S. Navy Photo)

Montana (BB-51)

NAME (HULL NO.)	BUILDER	KEEL LAID	LAUNCHED	COMMISSIONED
MONTANA (BB-51)	Mare I.	1 Sep 1920	NEVER	NEVER

Authorized 4 Mar 1917. Contract awarded 2 Jul 1918. Rated as BATTLESHIP NO. 51. Classified BB-51 on 17 Jul 1920. Construction suspended 8 Feb 1922 when 27.6% completed and cancelled 17 Aug 1923 in accordance with the terms of the Washington Treaty for Naval Limitations. Struck 24 Aug 1923 from the NVR. Sold 25 Oct 1923 to Learner & Rosenthal, Oakland, CA, for $47,110.00. Scrapped on the ways.

Montana BB-51 — Photograph taken, 3 January 1921, looking forward from an overhead crane while under construction by the Mare Island Navy Yard, Vallejo, CA. Note the aft double-bottom structure in the foreground. (U.S. Naval History and Heritage Command Photo)

NAME (HULL NO.)	BUILDER	KEEL LAID	LAUNCHED	COMMISSIONED
NORTH CAROLINA (BB-52)	Norfolk NY	12 Jan 1920	NEVER	NEVER

Authorized 1 Jul 1918. Contract awarded 2 Jul 1918. Rated as BATTLESHIP NO. 52. Classified BB-52 on 17 Jul 1920. Construction suspended 8 Feb 1922 when 36.7% completed and cancelled 17 Aug 1923 in accordance with the terms of the Washington Treaty for Naval Limitations. Struck 24 Aug 1923 from the NVR. Sold 25 Oct 1923. Scrapped on the ways.

North Carolina BB-52 — Photograph taken, 24 April 1920, looking aft from the bow while under construction by the Norfolk Navy Yard, Portsmouth, VA. (Official U.S. Navy Photo)

North Carolina BB-52 — Photograph taken, 29 June 1921, looking aft from number one barbette while under construction by the Norfolk Navy Yard, Portsmouth, VA. (Official U.S. Navy Photo)

Iowa (BB-53)

NAME (HULL NO.)	BUILDER	KEEL LAID	LAUNCHED	COMMISSIONED
IOWA (BB-53)	NNS&DD Co.	17 May 1920	NEVER	NEVER

Authorized 1 Jul 1918. Contract awarded 27 Oct 1919. Rated as BATTLESHIP NO. 53. Classified BB-53 on 17 Jul 1920. Construction suspended 8 Feb 1922 when 31.8% completed and cancelled 17 Aug 1923 in accordance with the terms of the Washington Treaty for Naval Limitations. Struck 24 Aug 1923 from the NVR. Sold 8 Nov 1923. Scrapped on the ways.

Left: *Iowa BB-53 — Photograph taken, 1 October 1921, looking forward from the stern while under construction by the Newport News Shipbuilding and Dry Dock Co., Newport News, VA. Note that the third deck was almost completely built. (Official U.S. Navy Photo)*

Below: *Iowa BB-53 — Photograph taken, 3 January 1922, looking forward from the stern while under construction by the Newport News Shipbuilding and Dry Dock Co., Newport News, VA. Note that number four barbette had been recently constructed. (Official U.S. Navy Photo)*

Class Specifications			As Designed (1920)
HULL	LENGTH	Waterline	660' 0"
		Overall	684' 0"
	EXTREME BEAM		105' 0"
	DISPLACE-MENT	Full Load	43,200 tons
		Normal	43,200 tons
	MAXIMUM DRAFT		33' 4"
	COMPLE-MENT	Officers	64
		Enlisted	1,281
ARMAMENT		Main	(4) triple 16"/50 turrets
		Secondary	(16) single 6"/53 mounts
			(4) single 3"/50 AA mounts
			(4) single 6 pdr. saluting
		Torpedo Tubes	(2) 21" submerged
ARMOR		Belt	8" – 13.5"
		Bulkheads	8" – 13.5"
		Deck	6"
		Turrets	9" – 18"
		Barbettes	4.5" – 13.5"
		Conning Tower	16"
ENGI-NEERING	SPEED	Maximum	23.0 knots
		Economical	10.0 knots
	ENGINES	Manufacturer	Westinghouse (BB-49 to 52)
			General Electric (BB-53, 54)
		Type	Turbo-Electric
	HORSE-POWER	Shaft	60,000
	SCREWS		4
	BOILERS	Manufacturer	White-Forster (BB-49, 50, 53)
			Bureau Express (BB-51, 52)
			Yarrow (BB-54)
		Type/No.	WT/12
	FUEL CAPACITY		6,600 tons oil
	DRIVE		TED

NAME (HULL NO.)	BUILDER	KEEL LAID	LAUNCHED	COMMISSIONED
MASSACHUSETTS (BB-54)	Beth., Ship	4 Apr 1921	NEVER	NEVER

Authorized 1 Jul 1918. Contract awarded 15 Nov 1919. Rated as BATTLESHIP NO. 54. Classified BB-54 on 17 Jul 1920. Construction suspended 8 Feb 1922 when 11.0% completed and cancelled 17 Aug 1923 in accordance with the terms of the Washington Treaty for Naval Limitations. Struck 24 Aug 1923 from the NVR. Sold 8 Nov 1923 to the Steel Scrap Co., Philadelphia, PA. Scrapped on the ways.

Massachusetts BB-54 — Photograph taken, 7 July 1921, while under construction by the Bethlehem Shipbuilding Corp, Quincy, MA. Note that on 1 April 1921, her keel was laid. (Official U.S. Navy Photo)

Massachusetts BB-54 — Photograph taken, 14 February 1922, after all work had been stopped on 8 February 1922, at the Bethlehem Shipbuilding Corp, Quincy, MA. Note that at this time, she was 11% complete. (Official U.S. Navy Photo)

22: NORTH CAROLINA CLASS (BB-55 to BB-56)

North Carolina (BB-55)

NAME (HULL NO.)	BUILDER	KEEL LAID	LAUNCHED	COMMISSIONED
NORTH CAROLINA (BB-55)	New York NY	27 Oct 1937	13 Jun 1940	9 Apr 1941

Authorized 27 Mar 1934. Contract awarded 24 Jun 1937. Sponsored by Miss Isabel Hoey. First Commanding Officer: CAPT Olaf M. Hustvedt. Decomm. 27 Jun 1947 at Brooklyn, NY. Struck 1 Jun 1960 from the NVR. Trans. 6 Sep 1961 to the State of North Carolina for use as a memorial at Wilmington, NC, where she remains berthed.

North Carolina BB-55 — Photographs taken, 17 April 1942, while underway at high speed at an unknown location along the East Coast of the United States. Note that she wore a Measure 12 Modified camouflage pattern. Also note that at this time there were no 40mm mounts and that she carried just a few 20 mm mounts. (Official U.S. Navy Photo)

North Carolina BB-55 — Photographs taken, 3 June 1942, anchored in Hampton Roads, VA, following her post-shakedown availability by the Norfolk Navy Yard, Portsmouth, VA. Note that she wore a Measure 12 Modified camouflage pattern and that her stern quad. 40 mm mounts had not yet been installed.

North Carolina BB-55 — Photograph taken, 24 January 1944, while underway at an unknown location in the Marshall Islands area of the Pacific Ocean. Note that she wore a Measure 32/18D early camouflage pattern. (Official U.S. Navy Photo)

North Carolina BB-55 — Photographs taken, 24 September 1944, anchored in Sinclair Inlet, WA, during an overhaul by the Puget Sound Navy Yard, Bremerton, WA. Note that she wore a Measure 32/18D late camouflage pattern. (Official U.S. Navy Photo)

Below: *North Carolina BB-55 — Photograph taken, 25 September 1944, while underway at high speed making 26 knots on sea trials in Puget Sound, WA, during an overhaul by the Puget Sound Navy Yard, Bremerton, WA. Note that she wore a Measure 32/18D late camouflage pattern. (Official U.S. Navy Photo)*

North Carolina BB-55 — Photograph taken, 5 October 1944, while underway at an unknown location along the West Coast of the United States. Note that she wore a Measure 32/18D late camouflage pattern and that all turrets were trained aft and to port. (Official U.S. Navy Photo)

North Carolina BB-55 — Photograph taken, 3 June 1946, while underway at an unknown location in the Atlantic Ocean following a refit by the New York Naval Shipyard, Brooklyn, NY. Note that she wore a Measure 22 camouflage pattern and that most of her light AA battery had been removed. (Official U.S. Navy Photo)

Washington (BB-56)

NAME (HULL NO.)	BUILDER	KEEL LAID	LAUNCHED	COMMISSIONED
WASHINGTON (BB-56)	Phil., NY	14 Jun 1938	1 Jun 1940	15 May 1941

Authorized 27 Mar 1934. Contract awarded 24 Jun 1937. Sponsored by Miss Virginia Marshall. First Commanding Officer: CAPT Howard H. J. Benson. Decomm. 27 Jun 1947 at Brooklyn, NY. Struck 1 Jun 1960 from the NVR. Sold 6 Jun 1961 to Lipsett Div., Luria Bros. & Co., Inc., New York City, NY, for $757,000.00. Scrapped.

Washington BB-56 — Photograph taken, 29 May 1941, while underway in the Delaware River off of the Philadelphia Navy Yard, Philadelphia, PA, 14 days after her commissioning. Note that she wore a Measure 1 camouflage pattern. (Official U.S. Navy Photo)

Washington BB-56 — Photograph taken, 21 August 1942, anchored in New York Harbor, NY, taking on stores following an overhaul by the New York Navy Yard, Brooklyn, NY. Note that she wore a Measure 22 camouflage pattern. (Official U.S. Navy Photo)

Washington BB-56 — Photograph taken, 2 April 1944, while underway on sea trials in Puget Sound, WA, during battle damage repairs by the Puget Sound Navy Yard, Bremerton, WA. On 1 February 1944, she collided with USS Indiana (BB-58) resulting in 60 feet of her bow being crumpled. (Official U.S. Navy Photo)

Washington BB-56 — Photographs taken, 26 April 1944, while underway in Sinclair Inlet, WA, following battle damage repairs by the Puget Sound Navy Yard, Bremerton, WA. On 1 February 1944, she collided with USS Indiana (BB-58) resulting in 60 feet of her bow being crumpled. Note that she wore a Measure 22 camouflage pattern. (Official U.S. Navy Photo)

Washington BB-56 — Photograph taken, 26 April 1944, while underway in Sinclair Inlet, WA, following battle damage repairs by the Puget Sound Navy Yard, Bremerton, WA. On 1 February 1944, she collided with USS Indiana (BB-58) resulting in 60 feet of her bow being crumpled. Note that she wore a Measure 22 camouflage pattern. (Official U.S. Navy Photo)

Class Specifications			As Completed (1941)
HULL	LENGTH	Waterline	714' 6" (BB-55)
			713' 8" (BB-56)
		Overall	728' 9" (BB-55)
			728' 11" (BB-56)
	EXTREME BEAM		108' 4" (BB-55)
			108' 0" (BB-56)
	DISPLACEMENT	Full Load	46,770 tons (BB-55)
			45,370 tons (BB-56)
		Standard	34,170 tons
	MAXIMUM DRAFT		35' 6" (BB-55)
			34' 9" (BB-56)
	COMPLEMENT	Officers	137 (BB-55)
			163 (BB-56)
		Enlisted	2,159 (BB-55)
			2,340 (BB-56)
ARMAMENT		Main	(3) triple 16"/45 turrets
		Secondary	(10) twin 5"/38 DP mounts
			(4) quad 1.1"/75 mounts
			(12) .50 cal. mg.
	ARMOR	Belt	6" – 12"
		Bulkheads	11.1" – 1.9"
		Deck	7"
		Turrets	9.8" – 16"
		Barbettes	16"
		5" Gun Mounts	1" – 1.5"
		5" Gun Barbettes	1.5"
		Conning Tower	16"
	AIRCRAFT	Number	3
		Catapults	(2) aft
ENGINEERING	SPEED	Maximum	27.0 knots
		Economical	15.0 knots
	ENGINES	Manufacturer	General Electric
		Type	Geared Turbines
	HORSEPOWER	Shaft	121,000
	SCREWS		4
	BOILERS	Manufacturer	B & W
		Type/No.	WT/8
	FUEL CAPACITY		6,592 tons oil (BB-55)
			6,583 tons oil (BB-56)
	DRIVE		TRD

Washington BB-56 — Photograph taken, 11 April 1945, while underway at high speed in a moderate sea. USS Hancock (CV-19) was to port of USS Washington (BB-56), as seen from USS Essex (CV-9). Note that she wore a Measure 22 camouflage pattern.

Washington BB-56 — Photograph taken, 10 September 1945, anchored in Puget Sound, WA, during her final overhaul by the Puget Sound Navy Yard, Bremerton, WA. Note that she wore a Measure 22 camouflage pattern. (Official U.S. Navy Photo)

Washington BB-56 — Photograph taken, 10 September 1945, while underway at high speed making 27.3 knots on sea trials in Puget Sound, WA, during her final overhaul by the Puget Sound Navy Yard, Bremerton, WA. Note that she wore a Measure 22 camouflage pattern. (Official U.S. Navy Photo)

23: SOUTH DAKOTA CLASS (BB-57 to BB-60)

South Dakota (BB-57)

NAME (HULL NO.)	BUILDER	KEEL LAID	LAUNCHED	COMMISSIONED
SOUTH DAKOTA (BB-57)	NY Ship Corp.	5 Jul 1939	7 Jun 1941	20 Mar 1942

Authorized 27 Mar 1934. Contract awarded 15 Dec 1938. Sponsored by Mrs. Harlan J. Bushfield. First Commanding Officer: CAPT Thomas L. Gatch. Originally named ALABAMA. Renamed SOUTH DAKOTA 28 Nov 1938. Decomm. 31 Jan 1947 at Philadelphia, PA. Struck 1 Jun 1962 from the NVR. Sold 25 Nov 1962 to Lipsett Div., Luria Bros, & Co., New York City, NY, for $466,665.00. Scrapped.

South Dakota BB-57 — Photograph taken, 1 October 1939, looking forward from frame 140, while under construction by the New York Shipbuilding Corp., Camden, NJ. Note the double-bottom structure starting forward and moving aft. (Official U.S. Navy Photo)

South Dakota BB-57 — Photograph taken, 1 October 1940, looking forward from frame 47, while under construction by the New York Shipbuilding Corp., Camden, NJ. Note the Class "A" Armor "No Welding" markings on the bulkhead just forward of number one barbette. (Official U.S. Navy Photo)

South Dakota BB-57 — Photograph taken, 1 January 1942, from the superstructure looking aft from frame 65, while being fitted out by the New York Shipbuilding Corp., Camden, NJ. (Official U.S. Navy Photo)

South Dakota BB-57 — Photograph taken, 1 January 1942, looking aft from frame 115, while being fitted out by the New York Shipbuilding Corp., Camden, NJ. Note the condition of turret number three as it was being assembled and the 16" dummy shells on the deck next to the gun barrel on the left. (Official U.S. Navy Photo)

South Dakota BB-57 — Photograph taken, February 1943, while underway in New York Harbor, NY, during her first refit by the New York Navy Yard, Brooklyn, NY, after receiving war damage in the Pacific. Note that she wore a Measure 21 camouflage pattern.

South Dakota BB-57 — Photograph taken, 20 August 1943, while underway in the Elizabeth River during her second refit by the Norfolk Navy Yard, Portsmouth, VA. Note that she wore a Measure 21 camouflage pattern. (Ray D. Bean photo collection)

South Dakota BB-57 — Photograph taken, 21 August 1944, while underway making 21 knots on sea trials in Puget Sound, WA, during an overhaul by the Puget Sound Navy Yard, Bremerton, WA. Note that she wore a Measure 21 camouflage pattern. (Official U.S. Navy Photo)

South Dakota BB-57 — Photographs taken, 24 August 1944, anchored in Sinclair Inlet, WA, following an overhaul by the Puget Sound Navy Yard, Bremerton, WA. Note that she wore a Measure 21 camouflage pattern. Also note that the number one turret was trained out to port, and the quad. 40 mm AA mounts, forward and on the bow. (Official U.S. Navy Photo)

South Dakota BB-57 — Photograph taken, 8 February 1945, anchored at fleet anchorage, Ulithi Atoll, Caroline Islands. Note that she wore a Measure 21 camouflage pattern. Also note that number three turret was trained out to starboard and the quad. 40 mm AA mounts, forward and on the bow. (Official U.S. Navy Photo)

Indiana (BB-58)

NAME (HULL NO.)	BUILDER	KEEL LAID	LAUNCHED	COMMISSIONED
INDIANA (BB-58)	NNS&DD Co.	20 Nov 1939	21 Nov 1941	30 Apr 1942

Authorized 27 Mar 1934. Contract awarded 15 Dec 1938. Sponsored by Mrs. Lewis C. Robbins. First Commanding Officer: CAPT Aaron S. Merrill. Decomm. 11 Sep 1947 at Bremerton, WA. Served as accommodation ship for the Bremerton Reserve Fleet until relieved by USS MISSOURI (BB-63) on 10 Mar 1955. Struck 1 Jun 1962 from the NVR. Sold 23 Oct 1963 to the Nicolai Joffe Corp., Beverly Hills, CA, for $418,387.13. Scrapped.

Indiana BB-58 — Photograph taken, 8 September 1942, anchored in Hampton Roads, VA. Note that she wore a Measure 12 Modified camouflage pattern. Also note that number one and three turrets were trained out to starboard and some of the crew over the side touching up the camouflage with some new paint. (Official U.S. Navy Photo)

Indiana BB-58 — Photograph taken, 17 December 1942, anchored at an unknown harbor in the South Pacific. Note that she wore a Measure 22 camouflage pattern.

Indiana BB-58 — Photographs taken, 30 November 1944, while underway at high speed, making a hard starboard turn on sea trials in Puget Sound, WA, during an overhaul by the Puget Sound Navy Yard, Bremerton, WA. (Official U.S. Navy Photo)

Indiana BB-58 — Photograph taken, 30 November 1944, while underway at high speed on sea trials in Puget Sound, WA, during an overhaul by the Puget Sound Navy Yard, Bremerton, WA. Note that she wore a Measure 22 camouflage pattern. (Official U.S. Navy Photo)

Indiana BB-58 — Photographs taken, 5 December 1944, anchored in Sinclair Inlet, WA, following an overhaul by the Puget Sound Navy Yard, Bremerton, WA. Note that she wore a Measure 22 camouflage pattern. (Official U.S. Navy Photo)

Indiana BB-58 — Photograph taken, 5 December 1944, anchored in Sinclair Inlet, WA, following an overhaul by the Puget Sound Navy Yard, Bremerton, WA. Note that she wore a Measure 22 camouflage pattern. (Official U.S. Navy Photo)

Indiana BB-58 — Photograph taken, circa 1945, while underway at an unknown location in the Pacific Ocean, heading home after the war's end.

Massachusetts (BB-59)

NAME (HULL NO.)	BUILDER	KEEL LAID	LAUNCHED	COMMISSIONED
MASSACHUSETTS (BB-59)	Beth., Quincy	20 Jul 1939	23 Sep 1941	12 May 1942

Authorized 27 Mar 1934. Contract awarded 15 Dec 1938. Sponsored by Mrs. Charles F. Adams. First Commanding Officer: CAPT Francis E. M. Whiting. Decomm. 27 Mar 1947 at Brooklyn, NY. Struck 1 Jun 1962 from the NVR. Trans. 4 Jun 1965 to the Massachusetts Memorial Committee for use as a memorial at Fall River, MA, where she remains berthed.

Massachusetts BB-59 — Photograph taken, 12 May 1942, while underway in Boston Harbor, Boston, MA, following her commission earlier that day. Note that she wore a Measure 12 Modified camouflage pattern. Also note that her stern quad. 40 mm mounts had not yet been installed, as well as the radars for the Mk. 37 gun directors. (Ray D. Bean photo collection)

Massachusetts BB-59 — Photographs taken, 11 July 1944, while underway in Sinclair Inlet, WA, during an overhaul by the Puget Sound Navy Yard, Bremerton, WA. Note that she wore a Measure 22 camouflage pattern. (Official U.S. Navy Photo)

Massachusetts BB-59 — Photograph taken, 11 July 1944, while underway in Sinclair Inlet, WA, during an overhaul by the Puget Sound Navy Yard, Bremerton, WA. Note that she wore a Measure 22 camouflage pattern. (Official U.S. Navy Photo)

Massachusetts BB-59 — Photographs taken, 11 July 1944, while underway, making 15 knots on sea trials off of Point Wilson, WA, during an overhaul by the Puget Sound Navy Yard, Bremerton, WA. Note that she wore a Measure 22 camouflage pattern and that her number one turret was trained out to starboard. (Official U.S. Navy Photo)

Massachusetts BB-59 — Photographs taken, 22 January 1946, while underway, making 6 knots on sea trials in Puget Sound, WA, during her final overhaul by the Puget Sound Naval Shipyard, Bremerton, WA. Note that she wore a Measure 22 camouflage pattern. (Official U.S. Navy Photo)

Massachusetts BB-59 — Photograph taken, circa June 1965, being towed in the Elizabeth River from the Norfolk Naval Shipyard, Portsmouth, VA, on her way to Fall River, MA, to become a museum ship. (Official U.S. Navy Photo)

Massachusetts BB-59 — Photograph taken, 12 June 1965, while underway being towed in Narraganset Bay, RI, on her way to Fall River, MA, to become a museum ship. (Official U.S. Navy Photo)

Alabama (BB-60)

NAME (HULL NO.)	BUILDER	KEEL LAID	LAUNCHED	COMMISSIONED
ALABAMA (BB-60)	Norfolk NY	1 Feb 1940	16 Feb 1942	16 Aug 1942

Authorized 27 Mar 1934. Contract awarded 1 Apr 1939. Sponsored by Mrs. Lister Hill. First Commanding Officer: CAPT George B. Wilson. Originally named SOUTH DAKOTA. Renamed ALABAMA 28 Nov 1938. Decomm. 9 Jan 1947 at Seattle, WA. Struck 1 Jun 1962 from the NVR. Trans. 16 Jun 1964 to the State of Alabama for use as a memorial at Mobile, AL, where she remains berthed.

Alabama BB-60 — Photograph taken, circa December 1942, anchored off of Casco Bay, ME, during her shakedown cruise. Note that she wore a Measure 12 Modified camouflage pattern. (Official U.S. Navy Photo)

Alabama BB-60 — Photograph taken, 1 December 1942, while underway off of Casco Bay, ME, during her shakedown cruise. Note that she wore a Measure 12 Modified camouflage pattern. Also note the two empty gun tubs on the main deck, beside the aft superstructure, and aft of number three turret. These were reserved for quad. 40 mm AA mounts that were in short supply at that time.

Alabama BB-60 — Photograph taken, 7 February 1943, anchored in the Elizabeth River during an availability period by the Norfolk Navy Yard, Portsmouth, VA. Note that she wore a Measure 22 camouflage pattern. (Official U.S. Navy Photo)

Alabama BB-60 — Photograph taken, 20 August 1943, while underway in the Elizabeth River following an overhaul by the Norfolk Navy Yard, Portsmouth, VA. Note that she wore a Measure 22 camouflage pattern. (Official U.S. Navy Photo)

Alabama BB-60 — Photograph taken, 1943–1944, while underway at an unknown location in the Pacific Ocean. Note that she wore a Measure 22 camouflage pattern. (Official U.S. Navy Photo)

Alabama BB-60 — Photograph taken, 12 March 1945, while underway on sea trials in Puget Sound, WA, during her final overhaul by the Puget Sound Naval Shipyard, Bremerton, WA. Note that she wore a Measure 22 camouflage pattern. (Official U.S. Navy Photo)

Alabama BB-60 — Photograph taken, 12 March 1945, while underway on sea trials in Puget Sound, WA, during her final overhaul by the Puget Sound Naval Shipyard, Bremerton, WA. Note that she wore a Measure 22 camouflage pattern. (Official U.S. Navy Photo)

Alabama BB-60 — Photograph taken, 15 March 1945, anchored in Sinclair Inlet, WA, during her final overhaul by the Puget Sound Naval Shipyard, Bremerton, WA. Note that she wore a Measure 22 camouflage pattern and the angles of the 16" barrels showing their independent elevation capabilities. (Official U.S. Navy Photo)

Alabama BB-60 — Photograph taken, 22 March 1945, while underway at an unknown location along the West Coast of the United States. Note that she wore a Measure 22 camouflage pattern. Also note that number one and three turrets were trained out to port, and number two turret trained out to starboard. (Official U.S. Navy Photo)

<table>
<tr><th colspan="3">Class Specifications</th><th>As Completed (1942)</th></tr>
<tr><td rowspan="11">HULL</td><td rowspan="2">LENGTH</td><td>Waterline</td><td>666’ 0”</td></tr>
<tr><td>Overall</td><td>680’ 0”</td></tr>
<tr><td colspan="2">EXTREME BEAM</td><td>108’ 2”</td></tr>
<tr><td rowspan="3">DISPLACEMENT</td><td rowspan="2">Full Load</td><td>44,374 tons (BB-57, 58, 60)</td></tr>
<tr><td>45,216 tons (BB-59)</td></tr>
<tr><td>Standard</td><td>35,000 tons</td></tr>
<tr><td colspan="2" rowspan="3">MAXIMUM DRAFT</td><td>36’ 4” (BB-57)</td></tr>
<tr><td>36’ 2” (BB-58, 60)</td></tr>
<tr><td>36’ 1” (BB-59)</td></tr>
<tr><td rowspan="2">COMPLEMENT</td><td>Officers</td><td>115</td></tr>
<tr><td>Enlisted</td><td>1,678</td></tr>
<tr><td rowspan="18">ARMAMENT</td><td rowspan="8"></td><td>Main</td><td>(3) triple 16”/45 turrets</td></tr>
<tr><td rowspan="7">Secondary</td><td>(8) twin 5”/38 DP mounts (BB-57)</td></tr>
<tr><td>(10) twin 5”/38 DP mounts (BB-58 to 60)</td></tr>
<tr><td>(7) quad 1.1”/75 mounts (BB-57)</td></tr>
<tr><td>(6) quad 40-mm mounts (BB-58 to 60)</td></tr>
<tr><td>(16) single 20-mm mounts (BB-58)</td></tr>
<tr><td>(22) single 20-mm mounts (BB-60)</td></tr>
<tr><td>(35) single 20-mm mounts (BB-59)</td></tr>
<tr><td rowspan="8">ARMOR</td><td>Belt</td><td>12.2”</td></tr>
<tr><td>Bulkheads</td><td>13.4”</td></tr>
<tr><td>Deck</td><td>8.25”</td></tr>
<tr><td>Turrets</td><td>9.5” – 18”</td></tr>
<tr><td>Barbettes</td><td>11.5” – 17.25”</td></tr>
<tr><td>5” Gun Mounts</td><td>1” – 1.5”</td></tr>
<tr><td>5” Gun Barbettes</td><td>1.5”</td></tr>
<tr><td>Conning Tower</td><td>15”</td></tr>
<tr><td rowspan="2">AIRCRAFT</td><td>Number</td><td>3</td></tr>
<tr><td>Catapults</td><td>(2) aft</td></tr>
<tr><td rowspan="13">ENGINEERING</td><td rowspan="2">SPEED</td><td>Maximum</td><td>27.0 knots</td></tr>
<tr><td>Economical</td><td>15.0 knots</td></tr>
<tr><td rowspan="3">ENGINES</td><td rowspan="2">Manufacturer</td><td>General Electric (BB-57, 59)</td></tr>
<tr><td>Westinghouse (BB-58, 60)</td></tr>
<tr><td>Type</td><td>Geared Turbines</td></tr>
<tr><td>HORSEPOWER</td><td>Shaft</td><td>130,000</td></tr>
<tr><td colspan="2">SCREWS</td><td>4</td></tr>
<tr><td rowspan="3">BOILERS</td><td rowspan="2">Manufacturer</td><td>B & W (BB-57, 59)</td></tr>
<tr><td>Foster-Wheeler (BB-58, 60)</td></tr>
<tr><td>Type/No.</td><td>WT/8</td></tr>
<tr><td colspan="2" rowspan="2">FUEL CAPACITY</td><td>6,950 tons oil (BB-57, 59)</td></tr>
<tr><td>7,340 tons oil (BB-58, 60)</td></tr>
<tr><td colspan="2">DRIVE</td><td>TRD</td></tr>
</table>

24: IOWA CLASS (BB-61 to BB-66)

Iowa (BB-61)

NAME (HULL NO.)	BUILDER	KEEL LAID	LAUNCHED	COMMISSIONED
IOWA (BB-61)	New York NY	27 Jun 1940	27 Aug 1942	22 Feb 1943

Authorized 17 May 1938. Contract awarded 1 Jul 1939. Sponsored by Mrs. Henry A. Wallace. First Commanding Officer: CAPT John L. McCrea. Decomm. 24 Mar 1949 at San Francisco, CA. Recomm. 25 Aug 1951. Decomm. 24 Feb 1958 at Philadelphia, PA. Recomm. 28 Apr 1984. Suffered major explosion in number two turret at 0955 on 19 Apr 1989 while conducting 16" gunnery firing exercises 330 miles off the Northeast Coast of Puerto Rico. Casualties: 47 dead. While all damage to the inside of number two turret and associated equipment was removed during a Restricted Availability (January 1990 – April 1990), at Norfolk Naval Shipyard, the turret itself was not repaired and remains completely inoperable. Decomm. 26 Oct 1990 at Norfolk Naval Operating Base, Norfolk, VA. Struck 12 Jan 1995 from the NVR. Reinstated 4 Jan 1999 on the NVR. Struck 25 Apr 2006 from the NVR. Donated 6 Sep 2011 to the Pacific Battleship Center, San Pedro, CA, for use as a museum and memorial at Berth 87, Port of Los Angeles, Los Angeles, CA.

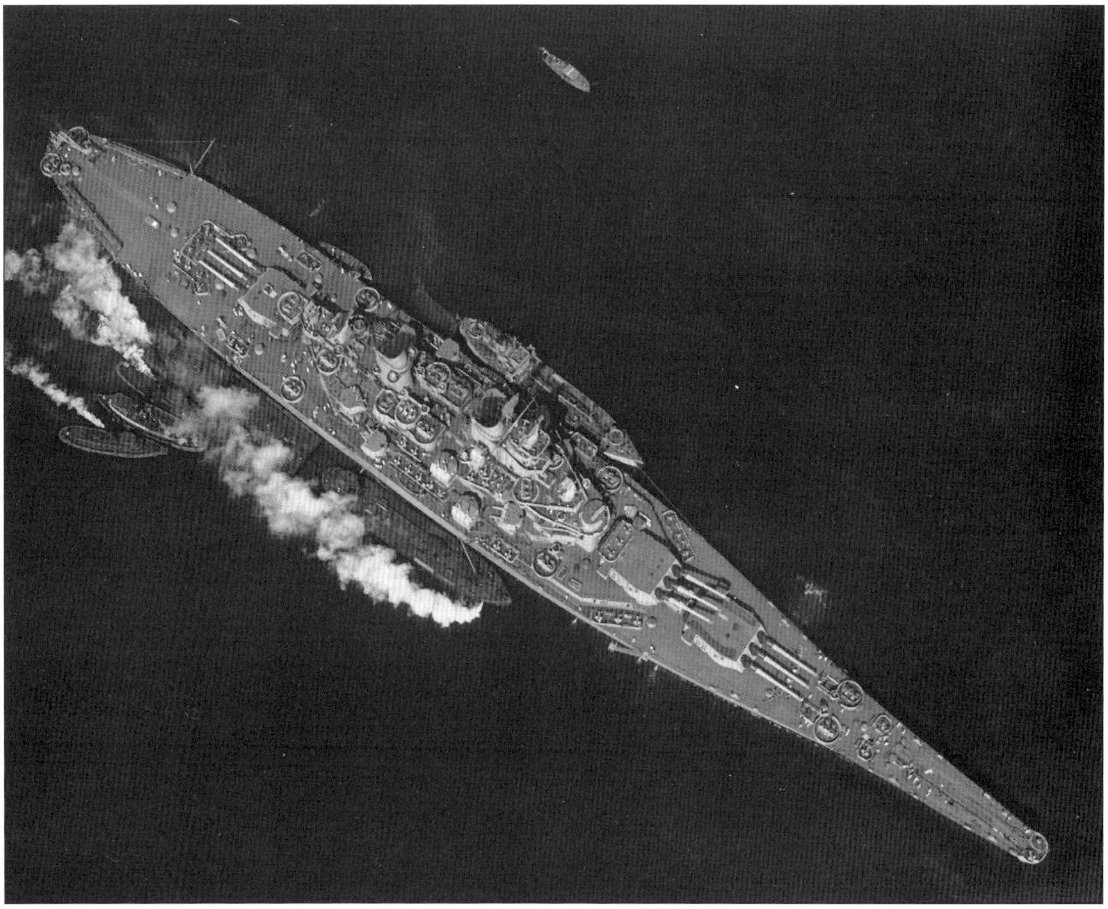

Iowa BB-61 — Photograph taken, 27 August 1943, anchored in Boston Harbor, Boston, MA. Note that she wore a Measure 22 camouflage pattern and all of the small craft tied up on both sides of her. (Official U.S. Navy Photo)

Iowa BB-61 — Photograph taken, 24 January 1944, while underway at an unknown location during the Marshall Islands campaign in the South Pacific. Note that she wore a Measure 32a/1B camouflage pattern. (Official U.S. Navy Photo)

Iowa BB-61 — Photograph taken, 27 December 1944, while underway approaching floating drydock USS ABSD-2 at Manus Island, Admiralty Islands, to fix shafting problems. Note that she wore a Measure 32a/1B camouflage pattern. (Official U.S. Navy Photo)

Iowa BB-61 — Photograph taken, 18 April 1952, while underway off of Wonsan Harbor, Korea. Note the helicopter sitting in the same area where her seaplanes would be during World War II. (Official U.S. Navy Photo)

Iowa BB-61 — Photograph taken, circa early 1984, while underway firing her main battery during sea trials in the Gulf of Mexico. Note the 16" shell in flight fired by number one turret, center gun barrel. (Official U.S. Navy Photo)

Iowa BB-61 — Photograph taken, December 1984, of the only bathtub in a modern U.S. Navy warship. It was installed as a convenience for President Franklin D. Roosevelt when he crossed the Atlantic Ocean for his conference at Casablanca, Morocco. (Official U.S. Navy Photo)

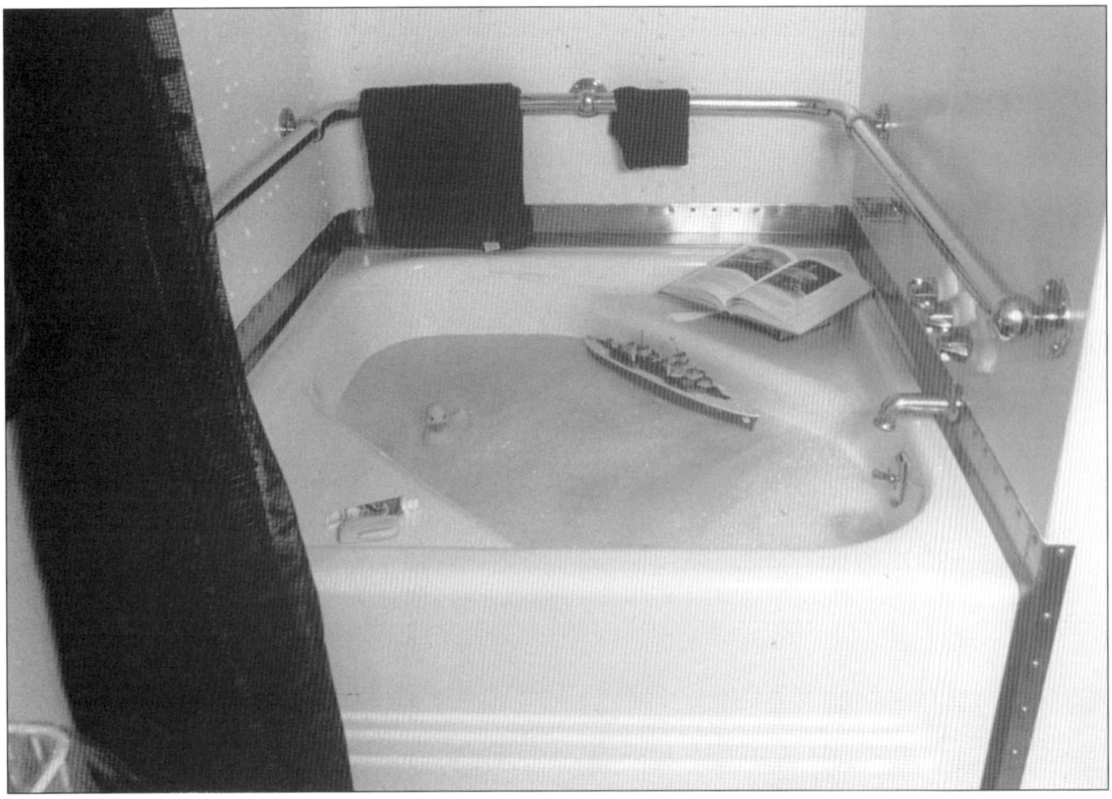

Iowa BB-61 — Photograph taken, 25 March 1985, while underway with weapons officer, CDR Richard Gano, discussing an ammunition off load with the Executive Officer CAPT John J. Chernesky (author's cousin), center, and the Commanding Officer CAPT Gerald E. Gneckow, right. Note that the 16" projectiles were staged on the deck for offloading. (Official U.S. Navy Photo)

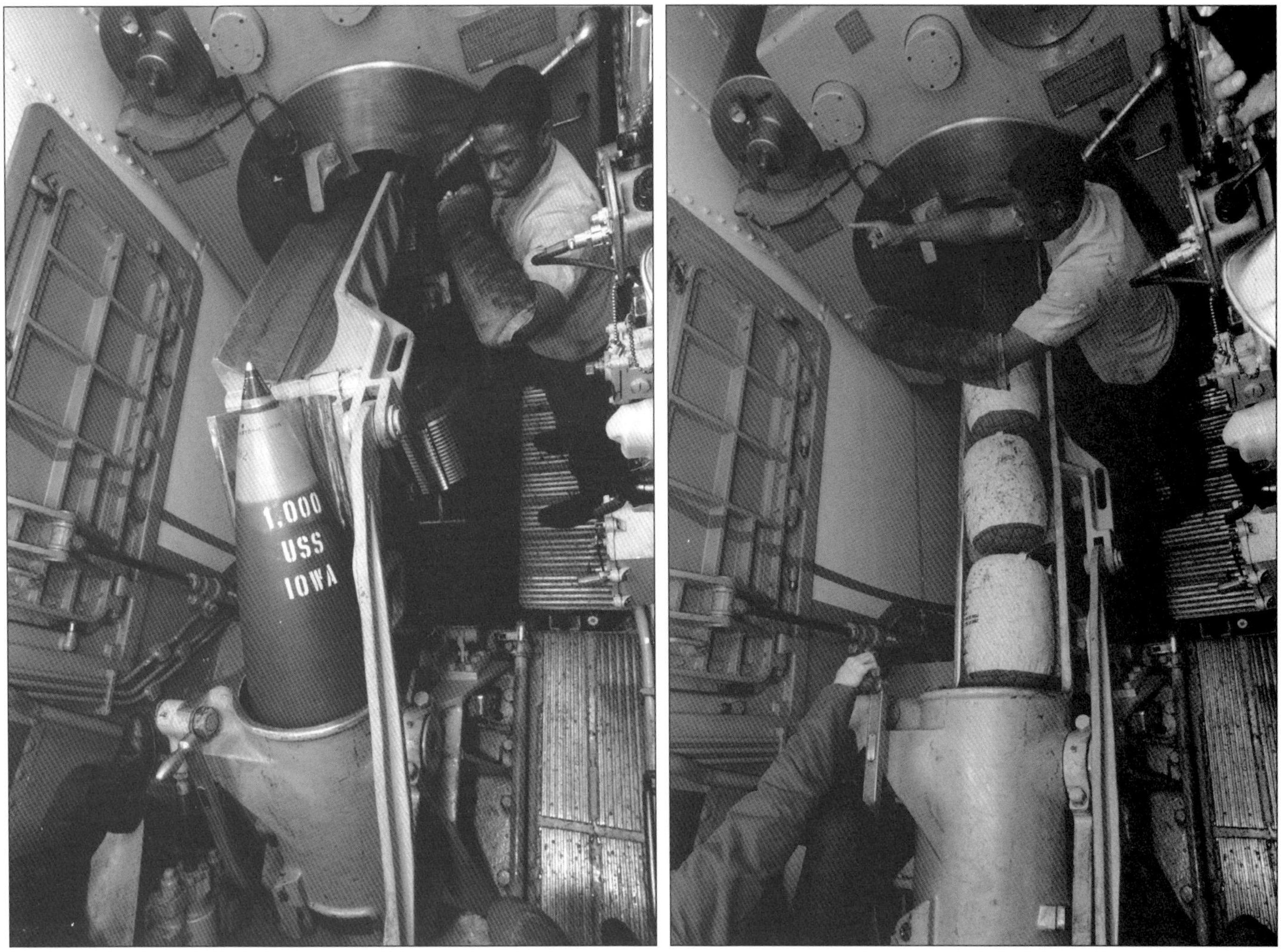

Iowa BB-61 — Photographs taken, 14 December 1986, while underway with a 1,900 pound high capacity (HC) projectile being hoisted up to the spanning tray in ***number*** *two turret, center gun barrel. Note that this particular projectile will be her 1,000th round fired by the 16" guns since recommissioning. (Official U.S. Navy Photo)*

Iowa BB-61 — Photograph taken, December 1988, while underway at an unknown location the Atlantic Ocean alongside USS Halyburton (FFG-40), as part of a NATO task group.

New Jersey (BB-62)

NAME (HULL NO.)	BUILDER	KEEL LAID	LAUNCHED	COMMISSIONED
NEW JERSEY (BB-62)	Phil., NY	16 Sep 1940	7 Dec 1942	23 May 1943

Authorized 17 May 1938. Contract awarded 1 Jul 1939. Sponsored by Mrs. Charles A. Edison. First Commanding Officer: CAPT Carl F. Holden. Decomm. 30 Jun 1948 at Bayonne, NJ. Recomm. 21 Nov 1950. Decomm. 21 Aug 1957 at Bayonne, NJ. Recomm. 6 Apr 1968. Decomm. 17 Dec 1969 at Bremerton, WA. Recomm. 28 Dec 1982. Decomm. 8 Feb 1991 at Long Beach, CA. Struck 12 Jan 1995 from the NVR. Reinstated 12 Feb 1998 on the NVR. Struck 4 Jan 1999 from the NVR. Donated 20 Jul 2000 to the Home Port Alliance, Camden, NJ, for use as a museum and memorial on the waterfront at Camden, NJ.

New Jersey BB-62 — Photograph taken, 12 October 1943, while underway in the Delaware River during her post-shakedown overhaul by the Philadelphia Navy Yard, Philadelphia, PA. Note that she wore a Measure 21 camouflage pattern and that her bridge has now been enclosed.

New Jersey BB-62 — Photograph taken, 8 February 1945, anchored at Ulithi Atoll, Caroline Islands. Note that she was in need of a refit and looks pretty forlorn with the paint peeling in splotches along the hull. (Ray D. Bean photo collection)

New Jersey BB-62 — Photograph taken, 30 June 1945, while underway in Puget Sound, WA, during an overhaul by the Puget Sound Navy Yard, Bremerton, WA. Note that she wore a Measure 22 camouflage pattern.

New Jersey BB-62 — Photograph taken, circa 1951–1953, while underway at an unknown location arriving in Korean waters. (Official U.S. Navy Photo)

New Jersey BB-62 — Photograph taken, April 1968, while underway at an unknown location in the Atlantic Ocean during her shakedown. Note the NTDS (Naval Tactical Data System) antenna mounted on the bow. (Ray D. Bean photo collection)

New Jersey BB-62 — Photograph taken, 17 June 1968, while underway in the Pacific Ocean, about five miles off the coast of San Diego, CA. (Ray D. Bean photo collection)

New Jersey BB-62 — Photograph taken, circa late 1968, while underway at an unknown location in the South China Sea during ammunition replenishment from USS Wrangell (AE-12). (Photograph taken by author)

New Jersey BB-62 — Photograph taken, circa late1968, while underway at an unknown location in the South China Sea during ammunition replenishment from USS Wrangell (AE-12). Note one of her swimming pools made from an old quad. 40 mm gun tub and painted aquamarine. (Photograph taken by author)

New Jersey BB-62 — Photograph taken, 12 June 1983, while underway entering Subic Bay, Philippines. Note the NTDS (Naval Tactical Data System) antenna mounted on the bow. (Official U.S. Navy Photo)

New Jersey BB-62 — Photograph taken, 11 August 1984, in dry dock during an overhaul by the Long Beach Naval Shipyard, Long Beach, CA. Note the condition of her hull and propellers. (Official U.S. Navy Photo)

Missouri (BB-63)

NAME (HULL NO.)	BUILDER	KEEL LAID	LAUNCHED	COMMISSIONED
MISSOURI (BB-63)	New York NY	6 Jan 1941	29 Jan 1944	11 Jun 1944

Authorized 17 May 1938. Contract awarded 12 Jun 1940. Sponsored by Miss Mary M. Truman. First Commanding Officer: CAPT William M. Callaghan. Ran aground 17 Jan 1950 at a point 1.6 miles from Thimble Shoals Light, near Old Point Comfort, in Hampton Roads, VA. Refloated 1 Feb 1950 with the aid of salvage ships and an incoming tide. Repaired at Norfolk Naval Shipyard. Decomm. 26 Feb 1955 at Bremerton, WA. Placed in service, in reserve, 10 Mar 1955 for use as accommodation/depot ship at the Bremerton Reserve Fleet, Bremerton, WA, relieving INDIANA (BB-58). Placed out of service, in reserve, December 1959 at Bremerton, WA, having been relieved by EURYALE (AS-22). Recomm. 10 May 1986. Decomm. 31 Mar 1992 at Long Beach, CA. Struck 12 Jan 1995 from the NVR. Donated 4 May 1998 to the MISSOURI Memorial Association, Honolulu, HI, for use as a museum and memorial adjacent to the ARIZONA at Ford Island.

Missouri BB-63 — Photograph taken, 24 July 1944, anchored in New York Harbor, NY, during her fitting out by the New York Navy Yard, Brooklyn, NY. Note that she wore a Measure 32/22D camouflage pattern. (Official U.S. Navy Photo)

Missouri BB-63 — Photograph taken, 30 July 1944, anchored in New York Harbor, NY, with a barge alongside during her fitting out by the New York Navy Yard, Brooklyn, NY. Note that she wore a Measure 32/22D camouflage pattern. (Official U.S. Navy Photo)

Missouri BB-63 — Photograph taken, 22 September 1944, while underway at an unknown location along the East Coast of the United States during battle practice. Note that she wore a Measure 32/22D camouflage pattern. (Official U.S. Navy Photo)

Missouri BB-63 — Photographs taken, 2 February 1950, in dry dock looking from frame 99 aft, during repairs by the Norfolk Naval Shipyard, Portsmouth, VA. On 17 January 1950, while underway in Hampton Roads, VA, she grounded at a point 1.6 miles from Thimble Shoals Light near Old Point Comfort. She was refloated on 1 February 1950. (Official U.S. Navy Photo)

Missouri BB-63 — Photograph taken, 2 February 1950, in dry dock cleaning out debris from her ripped open bottom, during repairs by the Norfolk Naval Shipyard, Portsmouth, VA. On 17 January 1950, while underway in Hampton Roads, VA, she grounded at a point 1.6 miles from Thimble Shoals Light near Old Point Comfort. She was refloated on 1 February 1950. (Official U.S. Navy Photo)

Missouri BB-63 — Photograph taken, August 1950, while underway at an unknown location in the Atlantic Ocean with USS Joseph P. Kennedy, Jr. (DD-850) alongside during refueling. (Ray D. Bean photo collection)

Missouri BB-63 — Photograph taken, October 1986, anchored in Sydney, Australia. Note the NTDS (Naval Tactical Data System) antenna mounted on the bow. (Official U.S. Navy Photo)

Missouri BB-63 — Photograph taken, October 1991, while underway at an unknown location along the West Coast of the United States. Note her hull number painted in white on top of number one turret and the NTDS (Naval Tactical Data System) antenna mounted on the bow. (Official U.S. Navy Photo)

Missouri BB-63 — Photograph taken, June 1998, tied up to a pier at Ford Island, HI, having just arrived there to become a museum ship. Note the NTDS (Naval Tactical Data System) antenna mounted on the bow. (Official Royal Australian Navy Photo)

Wisconsin (BB-64)

NAME (HULL NO.)	BUILDER	KEEL LAID	LAUNCHED	COMMISSIONED
WISCONSIN (BB-64)	Phil., NY	25 Jan 1941	7 Dec 1943	16 Apr 1944

Authorized 27 Mar 1934. Contract awarded 12 Jun 1940. Sponsored by Mrs. Walter S. Goodland. First Commanding Officer: CAPT Earl E. Stone. Decomm. 1 Jul 1948 at Norfolk, VA. Recomm. 3 Mar 1951. Collided with USS EATON (DDE-510) on 6 May 1954 off the Virginia Capes in a heavy fog. Received extensive bow damage. Repaired with bow from uncompleted KENTUCKY (BB-66). Decomm. 8 Mar 1958 at Bayonne, NJ. Recomm. 22 Oct 1988. Decomm. 30 Jun 1991 at Norfolk, VA. Struck 12 Jan 1995 from the NVR. Trans. to the Norfolk Inactive Fleet Facility, Portsmouth, VA. Arrived at Portsmouth, VA, 17 Oct 1996 having been towed from Philadelphia, PA. Reinstated 12 Feb 1998 on the NVR. Struck 17 Mar 2006 from the NVR. Donated 14 Dec 2009 to the City of Norfolk, VA, for use as a museum and memorial berthed adjacent to the Nauticus National Maritime Center, Norfolk, VA.

Wisconsin BB-64 — Photograph taken, 7 June 1944, while underway in the Delaware River off of the Philadelphia Navy Yard, Philadelphia, PA, during her shakedown. Note that she wore a Measure 22 camouflage pattern. (Official U.S. Navy Photo)

Wisconsin BB-64 — Photograph taken, 22 June 1944, while underway about 70 miles east of Virginia Beach, VA, in the Atlantic Ocean during her shakedown. Note that she wore a Measure 22 camouflage pattern. (Official U.S. Navy Photo)

Wisconsin BB-64 — Photograph taken, 24 September 1944, while underway in the Delaware River following her post-shakedown overhaul by the Philadelphia Navy Yard, Philadelphia, PA. Note that she wore a Measure 22 camouflage pattern. (Official U.S. Navy Photo)

Wisconsin BB-64 — Photograph taken, 27 March 1947, while underway from Cristobal, Panama Canal Zone.

Wisconsin BB-64 — Photograph taken, circa 1950s, while underway at an unknown location. (Official U.S. Navy Photo)

Wisconsin BB-64 — Photograph taken, circa 1957, while underway entering Hampton Roads, VA. (Ray D. Bean photo collection)

Wisconsin BB-64 — Photograph taken, 28 August 1988, while underway in the Gulf of Mexico, during her sea trials. Note the NTDS (Naval Tactical Data System) antenna mounted on the bow. (Official U.S. Navy Photo)

Wisconsin BB-64 — Photograph taken, 30 August 1988, while underway in the Gulf of Mexico, during her sea trials. Note the NTDS (Naval Tactical Data System) antenna mounted on the bow and her new helicopter landing deck. (Official U.S. Navy Photo)

Wisconsin BB-64 — Photograph taken, March 1991, while underway at an unknown location. Note the NTDS (Naval Tactical Data System) antenna mounted on the bow and the helicopter on deck aft. (Official U.S. Navy Photo)

Wisconsin BB-64 — Photograph taken, June 1991, while underway in an unknown harbor. Note the NTDS (Naval Tactical Data System) antenna mounted on the bow. (Official U.S. Navy Photo)

Illinois (BB-65)

NAME (HULL NO.)	BUILDER	KEEL LAID	LAUNCHED	COMMISSIONED
ILLINOIS (BB-65)	Phil., NY	15 Jan 1945	NEVER	NEVER

Authorized 19 Jul 1940. Contract awarded 9 Sep 1940. Construction cancelled 11 Aug 1945 when 21.0% completed. Uncompleted hulk considered for completion to an anti-aircraft battleship, but replaced by KENTUCKY (BB-66). Also considered for use as a target in the two atomic bomb tests at Bikini Atoll, Marshall Islands, but dropped due to state of incompletion. Broken up in September 1948 on the builders ways.

Illinois BB-65 — Photograph taken, 7 July 1945, while under construction looking from the stern forward at the Philadelphia Naval Shipyard, Philadelphia, PA. (Official U.S. Navy Photo)

NAME (HULL NO.)	BUILDER	KEEL LAID	LAUNCHED	COMMISSIONED
KENTUCKY (BB-66)	Norfolk NY	7 Mar 1942	20 Jan 1950	NEVER

Authorized 19 Jul 1940. Contract awarded 9 Sep 1940. Originally laid down 7 Mar 1942 on Builders Ways No. 1. Hull section floated off ways 10 Jun 1942 in order to make room for priority construction of landing craft. Hull section stored in a corner of the yard until 7 Dec 1944 when it was towed into Drydock No. 8 for resumption of construction. Keel officially re-laid 6 Dec 1944. Construction again suspended 17 Feb 1947. Construction resumed 17 Aug 1948 to clear the drydock. Unofficially launched 20 Jan 1950 when completed up to the 1st deck. Construction cancelled 20 Jan 1950 when 73.1% completed. Bow used to replace the damaged bow of USS WISCONSIN (BB-64). Various plans to complete the ship were considered including completion as a "Guided Missile Capital Ship (BBG)" but were dropped. Struck 9 Jun 1958 from the NVR. Sold 31 Oct 1958 to the Boston Metals Co., Baltimore, MD, for $1,176,666.00. Scrapped. During scrapping, the installed turbines were salvaged and returned to the Navy. After a complete overhaul, they were placed in storage and later installed in the USS SACRAMENTO (AOE-1) and the USS CAMDEN (AOE-2) during their construction.

Kentucky BB-66 — Photograph taken, February 1946, while under construction in a dry dock, looking from the bow aft at the Norfolk Naval Shipyard, Portsmouth, VA. (Official U.S. Navy Photo)

Kentucky BB-66 — Photograph taken, 11 September 1946, while under construction in a dry dock, looking from the bow aft, at the Norfolk Naval Shipyard, Portsmouth, VA. (Official U.S. Navy Photo)

Kentucky BB-66 — Photograph taken, 20 January 1950, being towed out of dry dock into the Elizabeth River at the Norfolk Naval Shipyard, Portsmouth, VA. The dry dock had to be cleared so that USS Missouri (BB-63) could be repaired following her grounding on 17 January 1950. (Official U.S. Navy Photo)

Kentucky BB-66 — Photograph taken, circa May/June 1956, when the bow was being removed by the Newport News Shipbuilding and Dry Dock Co., Newport News, VA. Her bow was used to repair the damaged USS Wisconsin (BB-64).

Kentucky BB-66 — Photograph taken, 24 October 1956, tied up to a pier at the Norfolk Naval Shipyard, Portsmouth, VA. Her bow was used to repair the damaged USS Wisconsin (BB-64). (Official U.S. Navy Photo)

Class Specifications			As Completed (1944/1945)	Operational Condition as of 1956
HULL	LENGTH	Waterline	860' 0"	860' 0"
HULL	LENGTH	Overall	887' 3" (BB-61, 63, 64)	887' 5" (BB-61, 63, 64)
HULL	LENGTH	Overall	887' 7" (BB-62)	888' 0" (BB-62)
HULL	EXTREME BEAM		108' 2" (BB-61, 63)	108' 2" (BB-61, 63)
HULL	EXTREME BEAM		108' 1" (BB-62)	108' 1" (BB-62)
HULL	EXTREME BEAM		108' 3" (BB-64)	108' 3" (BB-64)
HULL	DISPLACEMENT	Full Load	57,540 tons (BB-61, 63)	57,450 tons (BB-61, 63)
HULL	DISPLACEMENT	Full Load	57,216 tons (BB-62, 64)	57,216 tons (BB-62, 64)
HULL	DISPLACEMENT	Standard	45,000 tons	45,000 tons
HULL	MAXIMUM DRAFT		37' 9" (BB-61, 63)	37' 9" (BB-61, 63)
HULL	MAXIMUM DRAFT		38' 0" (BB-62, 64)	38' 0" (BB-62, 64)
HULL	COMPLEMENT	Officers	117	159 (BB-61, 63)
HULL	COMPLEMENT	Officers		180 (BB-62, 64)
HULL	COMPLEMENT	Enlisted	1,804	2,312 (BB-61, 63)
HULL	COMPLEMENT	Enlisted		2,574 (BB-62, 64)
ARMAMENT		Main	(3) triple 16"/50 turrets	(3) triple 16"/50 turrets
ARMAMENT		Secondary	(10) twin 5"/38 DP mounts	(10) twin 5"/38 DP mounts
ARMAMENT		Secondary	(15) quad 40-mm mounts (BB-61)	(15) quad 40-mm mounts (BB-61)
ARMAMENT		Secondary	(16) quad 40-mm mounts (BB-62)	(16) quad 40-mm mounts (BB-64)
ARMAMENT		Secondary	(20) quad 40-mm mounts (BB-63, 64)	(18) quad 40-mm mounts (BB-62)
ARMAMENT		Secondary	(60) single 20-mm mounts (BB-61, 62)	(20) quad 40-mm mounts (BB-63)
ARMAMENT		Secondary	(49) single 20-mm mounts (BB-63, 64)	(2) single 6 pdr. saluting (BB-61, 63, 64)
ARMAMENT		Secondary		(4) single 6 pdr. saluting (BB-62)
ARMAMENT	ARMOR	Belt	12.2"	12.2"
ARMAMENT	ARMOR	Bulkheads	11.2"	11.2"
ARMAMENT	ARMOR	Deck	8.75"	8.75"
ARMAMENT	ARMOR	Turrets	7.25" – 17"	7.25" – 17"
ARMAMENT	ARMOR	Barbettes	17.3"	17.3"
ARMAMENT	ARMOR	5" Gun Mounts	1" – 1.5"	1" – 1.5"
ARMAMENT	ARMOR	5" Gun Barbettes	1.5"	1.5"
ARMAMENT	ARMOR	Conning Tower	17.25"	17.25"
ARMAMENT	AIRCRAFT	Number	3	None
ARMAMENT	AIRCRAFT	Catapults	(2) aft	None
ENGINEERING	SPEED	Maximum	32.5 knots	32.5 knots
ENGINEERING	SPEED	Economical	15.0 knots	15.0 knots
ENGINEERING	ENGINES	Manufacturer	General Electric (BB-61, 63, 66)	General Electric (BB-61, 63)
ENGINEERING	ENGINES	Manufacturer	Westinghouse (BB-62, 64, 65)	Westinghouse (BB-62, 64)
ENGINEERING	ENGINES	Type	Geared Turbines	Geared Turbines
ENGINEERING	HORSEPOWER	Shaft	212,000	212,000
ENGINEERING	SCREWS		4	4
ENGINEERING	BOILERS	Manufacturer	B & W	B & W
ENGINEERING	BOILERS	Type/No.	WT/8	WT/8
ENGINEERING	FUEL CAPACITY		7,073 tons oil (BB-61)	7,073 tons oil (BB-61)
ENGINEERING	FUEL CAPACITY		7,251 tons oil (BB-62 to 64)	7,251 tons oil (BB-62 to 64)
ENGINEERING	DRIVE		TRD	TRD

Class Specifications			NEW JERSEY (BB-62) 1968	Operational Condition as of 1988
HULL	LENGTH	Waterline	860' 0"	860' 0"
		Overall	888' 0"	887' 5" (BB-61, 63, 64)
				888' 0" (BB-62)
	EXTREME BEAM		108' 2"	108' 2"
	DISPLACEMENT	Full Load	59,000 tons	57,370 tons
		Standard	45,000 tons	48,425 tons
	MAXIMUM DRAFT		38' 0"	38' 0"
	COMPLEMENT	Officers	70	65
		Enlisted	1,556	1,450
		Marines		
		Officers	None	2
		Enlisted		38
ARMAMENT		Guns	(3) triple 16"/50 turrets	(3) triple 16"/50 turrets
			(10) twin 5"/38 DP mounts	(6) twin 5"/38 DP mounts
			(2) single 40-mm saluting	(4) 20-mm Phalanx CWIS
		Missiles	(4) single ZUNI rocket launchers	(4) quad HARPOON SSM launch canisters
				(8) quad TOMAHAWK TASM/TLAM launch canisters
	ARMOR	Belt	12.2"	12.2"
		Bulkheads	11.2"	11.2"
		Deck	8.75"	8.75"
		Turrets	7.25" – 17"	7.25" – 17"
		Barbettes	17.3"	17.3"
		5" Gun Mounts	1" – 1.5"	1" – 1.5"
		5" Gun Barbettes	1.5"	1.5"
		Conning Tower	17.25"	17.25"
ENGINEERING	SPEED	Maximum	32.5 knots	33.0 knots
		Economical	15.0 knots	15.0 knots
	ENGINES	Manufacturer	Westinghouse	General Electric (BB-61, 63)
				Westinghouse (BB-62, 64)
		Type	Geared Turbines	Geared Turbines
	HORSEPOWER	Shaft	212,000	212,000
	SCREWS		4	4
	BOILERS	Manufacturer	B & W	B & W
		Type/No.	WT/8	WT/8
	FUEL CAPACITY		7,251 tons oil	7,073 tons oil (BB-61)
				7,251 tons oil (BB-62 to 64)
	DRIVE		TRD	TRD

25: MONTANA CLASS (BB-67 to BB-71)

Montana (BB-67)

NAME (HULL NO.)	BUILDER	KEEL LAID	LAUNCHED	COMMISSIONED
MONTANA (BB-67)	Phil., NY	NEVER	NEVER	NEVER

Authorized 19 Jul 1940. Contract awarded 9 Sep 1940. Construction suspended 20 May 1942 and cancelled 21 Jul 1943.

Ohio (BB-68)

NAME (HULL NO.)	BUILDER	KEEL LAID	LAUNCHED	COMMISSIONED
OHIO (BB-68)	Phil., NY	NEVER	NEVER	NEVER

Authorized 19 Jul 1940. Contract awarded 9 Sep 1940. Construction suspended 20 May 1942 and cancelled 21 Jul 1943.

Maine (BB-69)

NAME (HULL NO.)	BUILDER	KEEL LAID	LAUNCHED	COMMISSIONED
MAINE (BB-69)	New York NY	NEVER	NEVER	NEVER

Authorized 19 Jul 1940. Contract awarded 9 Sep 1940. Was to be fitted as Fleet Flagship. Construction suspended 20 May 1942 and cancelled 21 Jul 1943.

New Hampshire (BB-70)

NAME (HULL NO.)	BUILDER	KEEL LAID	LAUNCHED	COMMISSIONED
NEW HAMPSHIRE (BB-70)	New York NY	NEVER	NEVER	NEVER

Authorized 19 Jul 1940. Contract awarded 9 Sep 1940. Construction suspended 20 May 1942 and cancelled 21 Jul 1943.

Louisiana (BB-71)

NAME (HULL NO.)	BUILDER	KEEL LAID	LAUNCHED	COMMISSIONED
LOUISIANA (BB-71)	Norfolk NY	NEVER	NEVER	NEVER

Authorized 19 Jul 1940. Contract awarded 9 Sep 1940. Construction suspended 20 May 1942 and cancelled 21 Jul 1943.

Class Specifications			Final Design
HULL	LENGTH	Waterline	890’ 0”
		Overall	921’ 3”
	EXTREME BEAM		121’ 2”
	DISPLACEMENT	Full Load	70,783 tons (BB-67, 68, 70, 71)
			70,965 tons (BB-69)
		Light	57,414 tons (BB-67, 68, 70, 71)
			57,534 tons (BB-69)
	MAXIMUM DRAFT		36’ 2”
	COMPLEMENT	Officers	115 (BB-67, 68, 70, 71)
			189 (BB-69)
		Enlisted	2,240 (BB-67, 68, 70, 71)
			2,789 (BB-69)
ARMAMENT		Main	(4) triple 16”/50 turrets
		Secondary	(10) twin 5”/54 mounts
			(10) quad 40-mm mounts
			(56) single 20-mm mounts
	ARMOR	Belt	16.1”
		Bulkheads	
		Forward	18”
		Aft	15.25”
		Deck	9.9”
		Turrets	18”
		Barbettes	7.25” – 21.3”
		5” Gun Mounts	1” – 1.5”
		5” Gun Barbettes	1”
		Conning Tower	18”
	AIRCRAFT	Number	3
		Catapults	(2) aft
ENGINEERING	SPEED	Maximum	28.0 knots
		Economical	15.0 knots
	ENGINES	Manufacturer	Westinghouse
		Type	Geared Turbines
	HORSEPOWER	Shaft	172,000
	SCREWS		4
	BOILERS	Manufacturer	B & W
		Type/No.	WT/8
	FUEL CAPACITY		7,500 tons oil
	DRIVE		TRD

"New Navy" Monitors

1: PURITAN CLASS (BM-1)

Puritan "(BM-1)"

NAME (HULL NO.)	BUILDER	KEEL LAID	LAUNCHED	COMMISSIONED
PURITAN "(BM-1)"	John Roach	May 1876	6 Dec 1882	10 Dec 1896

Authorized 3 Mar 1885 together with Acts of 3 Aug 1886 and 3 Mar 1887. Sponsored by Miss Fales. First Commanding Officer: CAPT John R. Bartlett. Rated as MONITOR NO. 1. Construction suspended from 1877–1882. Completed by New York Navy Yard. Placed in comm., in reserve, 18 Oct 1898 at Annapolis, MD. Decomm. 1 Mar 1899 at Annapolis, MD. Recomm. 10 Dec 1901. Decomm. 16 Apr 1903 at Philadelphia, PA. Recomm. 2 Jun 1903 to serve as a receiving ship at League Island, PA. Decomm. 16 Nov 1903 at Philadelphia, PA, and loaned to the District of Columbia Naval Militia until 14 Sep 1906. Decomm. 23 Apr 1910 at Norfolk, VA. Struck 27 Feb 1913 from the NVR. Employed as "Target B" from 1910–1917. Never assigned hull number BM-1. Would have been, had PURITAN still been on the NVR. Sold 26 Jan 1922 to Mr. Joseph G. Hitner & Mr. William F. Cutler, Philadelphia, PA. Scrapped.

Puritan BM-1 — Photograph taken, between December 1896 and early 1897, while underway at an unknown location along the Northeast Coast of the United States.

Puritan BM-1 — Photograph taken, between December 1896 and early 1897, while underway at an unknown location along the East Coast of the United States. (Official U.S. Navy Photo)

Class Specifications			As Completed (1896)
HULL	LENGTH	Waterline	290' 3"
		Overall	296' 3"
	EXTREME BEAM		60' 1.5"
	DISPLACEMENT	Normal	6,060 tons
	MEAN DRAFT		18' 0"
	COMPLEMENT	Officers	19
		Enlisted	210
ARMAMENT		Main	(2) twin 12"/35 B.L.R. turrets
		Secondary	(6) single 4"/40 R.F. mounts
			(6) single 6 pdr.
			(2) single 1 pdr.
	ARMOR	Belt	
		Top	14"
		Bottom	6"
		Waterline	14"
		Deck	2"
		Turrets	8"
		Barbettes	14"
		Conning Tower	10"
ENGINEERING	SPEED	Maximum	12.0 knots
		Economical	10.0 knots
	ENGINES	Manufacturer	John Roach
		Type	Horizontal Compound
	HORSEPOWER	Indicated	3,700
	SCREWS		2
	BOILERS	Manufacturer	John Roach
		Type/No.	Single-Ended Cylindrical/8
	FUEL CAPACITY		306 tons coal

2: AMPHITRITE CLASS (BM-2 to BM-5)

Amphitrite "(BM-2)"

NAME (HULL NO.)	BUILDER	KEEL LAID	LAUNCHED	COMMISSIONED
AMPHITRITE "(BM-2)"	Harlan	1874	7 Jun 1883	23 Apr 1895

Authorized 3 Mar 1885 together with Acts of 3 Aug 1886 and 3 Mar 1887. Sponsored by Miss Nellie Benson. First Commanding Officer: CAPT William C. Wise. Originally named TONAWANDA. Renamed AMPHITRITE 15 Jun 1869. Rated as MONITOR NO. 2. Completed by Norfolk Navy Yard. Placed in ordinary May 1897 at Norfolk, VA, for service as an instruction ship for gun captains. Recomm. 2 Oct 1897. Decomm. 30 Nov 1901 at Boston, MA. Recomm. 1 Dec 1902. Decomm. 3 Aug 1907 at Philadelphia, PA. Placed in comm., in reserve, 14 Jun 1910 for use as Naval Reserve training ship at St. Louis, MO. Reassigned 12 May 1912 for further service as a training ship by the Louisiana Naval Militia at New Orleans, LA. Reassigned 12 May 1916 to the Connecticut Naval Militia, based at New Haven, CT. Assigned 27 Apr 1917 to the 3rd Naval District for service as a guardship in New York City Harbor. Decomm. 13 May 1919 at Philadelphia, PA. Struck 24 Jul 1919 from the NVR. Sold 3 Jan 1920 to Mr. A. L. D. Bucksten, Elizabeth City, NC. Never assigned hull number BM-2. Would have been, had AMPHITRITE still been on the NVR. Stripped of her turrets and superstructure, she was used as a floating hotel at Beaufort, SC, and later in Florida. Chartered in 1943 by the U.S. Navy, and employed as a barracks ship for workers constructing a new Naval Air Station at Elizabeth City, NC. Towed to Baltimore, MD, in Spring 1950. Moved to a slip at Sandy Point, MD, for use as a floating restaurant and hotel. Sold again in 1951 and towed to Baltimore, MD. She was to be refitted as a barracks ship for workers in Venezuelan Oil Exploration, but was dropped and the ship was sold for scrapping in early 1952 to the Patapsco Steel Corp., Baltimore, MD. Scrapped by the Spring of 1952.

Amphitrite BM-2 — Photograph taken, circa 1895–1896, while underway in an unknown harbor along the East Coast of the United States. (Official U.S. Navy Photo)

Amphitrite BM-2 — Photograph taken, circa 1896, tied up to a pier at the Boston Navy Yard, Boston, MA.

Amphitrite BM-2 — Photograph taken, circa 1895–1902, anchored in an unknown harbor along the East Coast of the United States. Note the crew's laundry drying from lines rigged from the bow to the foremast and the canvas tarps rigged over the forward and aft parts of the ship. (Official U.S. Navy Photo)

Amphitrite BM-2 — Photograph taken, circa 1895–1902, while underway in an unknown harbor along the East Coast of the United States. Note the canvas tarps rigged over the forward and aft parts of the ship. (Official U.S. Navy Photo)

Amphitrite BM-2 — Photograph taken, early 1952, while being cut up for scrap in Baltimore, MD, having been used as a floating hotel and casino off the coast of Maryland in 1950–1951.

Monadnock (BM-3)

NAME (HULL NO.)	BUILDER	KEEL LAID	LAUNCHED	COMMISSIONED
MONADNOCK (BM-3)	Phineas	15 Jan 1875	19 Sep 1883	20 Feb 1896

Authorized 3 Mar 1885 together with Acts of 3 Aug 1886 and 3 Mar 1887. Sponsored by Miss Lulu Irwin. First Commanding Officer: CAPT George W. Sumner. Rated as MONITOR NO. 3. Construction suspended 1877–1882. Completed by Mare Island Navy Yard. Decomm. 10 Mar 1909 at Cavite, Philippines. Placed in comm., in reserve, 20 Apr 1911. Placed in full comm. 31 Jan 1912. Placed in comm., in reserve, 11 Feb 1913 at Olongapo, Philippines. Decomm. 25 Mar 1919. Classified BM-3 on 17 Jul 1920. Reclass. UNCLASSIFIED VESSEL, IX-17 on 21 Jul 1921. Struck 2 Feb 1923 from the NVR. Sold 24 Aug 1923 to Edward J. Nell & Co., Manila, Philippines for $10,250.00. Scrapped.

Monadnock BM-3 — Picture taken, circa 1896, anchored off of the Mare Island Navy Yard, Vallejo, CA. (Ray D. Bean photo collection)

Monadnock BM-3 — Picture taken, circa 1896–1901, while underway in San Francisco Bay, CA. (Official U.S. Navy Photo)

Terror "(BM-4)"

NAME (HULL NO.)	BUILDER	KEEL LAID	LAUNCHED	COMMISSIONED
TERROR "(BM-4)"	W. Cramp	1874	24 Mar 1883	15 Apr 1896

Authorized 3 Mar 1885 together with Acts of 3 Aug 1886 and 3 Mar 1987. Sponsored by Miss Martha Hichborn. First Commanding Officer: CAPT Purnell F. Harrington. Originally named AGAMENTICUS. Renamed TERROR 15 Jun 1869. Rated as MONITOR NO. 4. Construction suspended 1877–1882. Completed by New York Navy Yard. Placed in comm., in reserve, 18 Oct 1898 at Norfolk, VA. Decomm. 25 Feb 1899 at Norfolk, VA. Recomm. 10 May 1905. Placed in comm., in reserve, 11 Sep 1905 at Philadelphia, PA. Decomm. 8 May 1906 at Philadelphia, PA. Struck 15 Dec 1915 from the NVR. Designated as "Target D" 1 Jun 1916. Never assigned hull number BM-4. Would have been, had TERROR still been on the NVR. Sold 10 Mar 1921 to the U. S. Rail & Salvage Corp. Sunk on an undetermined date off Shooters Island, NY. Raised and broken up in 1930.

Terror BM-4 — Photograph taken, 23 April 1897, anchored off of New York City, NY. (Ray D. Bean photo collection)

Miantonomoh "(BM-5)"

NAME (HULL NO.)	BUILDER	KEEL LAID	LAUNCHED	COMMISSIONED
MIANTONOMOH "(BM-5)"	John Roach	1874	5 Dec 1876	27 Oct 1891

Authorized 3 Mar 1885 together with Acts of 3 Aug 1886 and 3 Mar 1887. Sponsored by Master Hiram Paulding. First Commanding Officer: CAPT Montgomery Sicard. Construction suspended 1877–1882. Comm. in an uncompleted condition 6 Oct 1882 and steamed to the New York Navy Yard for completion. Decomm. there 13 Mar 1883. Rated as MONITOR NO. 5. Decomm. 20 Nov 1895 at Philadelphia, PA. Recomm. 10 Mar 1898. Decomm. 8 Mar 1899 at Philadelphia, PA. Recomm. 9 Apr 1907. Decomm. 21 Dec 1907 at Philadelphia, PA. Struck 15 Dec 1915 from the NVR. Designated as "Target C". Never assigned hull number BM-5. Would have been, had MIANTONOMOH still been on the NVR. Sold 26 Jan 1922 to Mr. Joseph G. Hitner & Mr. William F. Cutler, Philadelphia, PA. Scrapped.

Miantonomoh BM-5 — Photograph taken, circa 1892, anchored in St. John, New Brunswick, Canada.

Class Specifications			As Completed (1891/1896)
HULL	LENGTH	Waterline	259’ 3” (BM-2)
			258’ 6” (BM-3)
			258’ 8” (BM-4)
			260’ 3” (BM-5)
		Overall	262’ 9” (BM-2)
			262’ 3” (BM-3)
			263’ 1” (BM-4, 5)
	EXTREME BEAM		55’ 4” (BM-2, 5)
			55’ 5” (BM-3)
			55’ 6” (BM-4)
	DISPLACEMENT	Normal	3,990 tons
	MEAN DRAFT		14’ 6” (BM-2, 3, 5)
			14’ 8” (BM-4)
	COMPLEMENT	Officers	19
		Enlisted	115 (BM-2)
			210 (BM-3, 4)
			164 (BM-5)
ARMAMENT		Main	(2) twin 10”/30 B.L.R. turrets
		Secondary	(2) single 4”/40 R.F. mounts (BM-2, 4)
			(4) single 6 pdr.
	ARMOR	Belt	
		Top	9” (BM-2, 3)
			7” (BM-4, 5)
		Bottom	4” (BM-2, 4, 5)
			5” (BM-3)
		Waterline	9” (BM-2, 3)
			7” (BM-4, 5)
		Deck	1.75”
		Turrets	7.1” (BM-2)
			7.5” (BM-3)
			11.5” (BM-4, 5)
		Barbettes	11.5” (BM-2, 3)
		Conning Tower	9”
ENGINEERING	SPEED	Maximum	10.5 knots (BM-2, 4, 5)
			10.63 knots (BM-3)
		Economical	10.0 knots
	ENGINES	Manufacturer	Harlan & Hollingsworth (BM-2)
			Continental Iron (BM-3)
			Cramp (BM-4)
			John Roach (BM-5)
		Type	Inclined Compound (BM-2, 4, 5)
			Horizontal 3-Exp. (BM-3)
	HORSEPOWER	Indicated	1,600 (BM-2, 4)
			2,163 (BM-3)
			1,426 (BM-5)
	SCREWS		2
	BOILERS	Manufacturer	B & W (BM-2)
			Continental Iron (BM-3)
			Cramp (BM-4)
			John Roach (BM-5)
		Type/No.	Single-Ended Cylindrical/ 4 (BM-2, 3)
			Single-Ended Cylindrical/ 6 (BM-4, 5)
	FUEL CAPACITY		271 tons coal (BM-2)
			386 tons coal (BM-3)
			276 tons coal (BM-4)
			250 tons coal (BM-5)

NAME (HULL NO.)	BUILDER	KEEL LAID	LAUNCHED	COMMISSIONED
MONTEREY (BM-6)	Union Iron	20 Dec 1889	28 Apr 1891	13 Feb 1893

Authorized 3 Mar 1887. Contract awarded 14 Jun 1889. Sponsored by Miss Kate C. Gunn. First Commanding Officer: CAPT Lewis Kemp. Rated as MONITOR NO. 6. Decomm. 15 Dec 1904 at Cavite, Philippines. Placed in comm., in reserve, 28 Sep 1907. Placed in ordinary 7 May 1908 at Olongapo, Philippines. Recomm. 9 Nov 1911. Decomm. 11 Feb 1913 at Olongapo, Philippines. Recomm. 21 Jun 1915. Classified BM-6 on 17 Jul 1920. Decomm. 27 Aug 1921 at Pearl Harbor, HI. Sold 25 Feb 1922 to the A. Bercovich Co., Oakland, CA. Scrapped.

Monterey BM-6 — Photograph taken, 1893–1901, while underway in an unknown port along the West Coast of the United States. (Official U.S. Navy Photo)

Monterey BM-6 — Photograph taken, circa 1913, anchored at Olongapo, Philippines. (Ray D. Bean photo collection)

Class Specifications			As Completed (1893)
HULL	LENGTH	Waterline	256' 0"
		Overall	260' 11"
	EXTREME BEAM		59' 0.5"
	DISPLACEMENT	Normal	4,084 tons
	MEAN DRAFT		14" 10"
	COMPLEMENT	Officers	21
		Enlisted	172
ARMAMENT		Main	(1) twin 12"/35 B.L.R. turret
			(1) twin 10"/30 B.L.R. turret
		Secondary	(6) single 6 pdr.
			(4) single 1 pdr.
	ARMOR	Belt	
		Top	13"
		Bottom	5"
		Waterline	13"
		Deck	2.5"
		12" Gun Turret	8"
		10" Gun Turret	7.5"
		12" Gun Barbette	13"
		10" Gun Barbette	11.5"
		Conning Tower	10"
ENGINEERING	SPEED	Maximum	13.6 knots
		Economical	10.0 knots
	ENGINES	Manufacturer	Union
		Type	Vert. 3-Exp. Recip.
	HORSEPOWER	Indicated	5,244
	SCREWS		2
	BOILERS	Manufacturer	B & W
		Type/No.	FT (Scotch)/4
	FUEL CAPACITY		206 tons coal

4: ARKANSAS CLASS (BM-7 to BM-10)

Arkansas (BM-7)

NAME (HULL NO.)	BUILDER	KEEL LAID	LAUNCHED	COMMISSIONED
ARKANSAS (BM-7)	NNS&DD Co.	14 Nov 1899	10 Nov 1900	28 Oct 1902

Authorized 4 May 1898. Contract awarded 11 Oct 1898. Sponsored by Miss Bobbie N. Jones. First Commanding Officer: CDR Charles E. Vreeland. Rated as MONITOR NO. 7. Placed in comm., in reserve, 11 Sep 1906 at Annapolis, MD. Placed in full comm. 4 Jun 1907. Placed in comm., in reserve, 31 Aug 1907 at Annapolis, MD. Placed in full comm. 1 Jun 1908. Placed in comm., in reserve, 1 Sep 1908 at Annapolis, MD. Renamed OZARK 2 Mar 1909. Assigned on 10 Jun 1910 as a training ship for the District of Columbia Naval Militia. Decomm. 20 Aug 1919 at Philadelphia, PA. Classified BM-7 on 17 Jul 1920. Struck 1 Jul 1921 from the NVR. Sold 26 Jan 1922. Scrapped.

Arkansas BM-7 — Photograph taken, 1902–1909, anchored in an unknown harbor along the East Coast of the United States. (Official U.S. Navy Photo)

Ozark BM-7 — Photograph taken, 1909–1914, tied up to a mooring buoy in an unknown harbor along the East Coast of the United States.

Ozark BM-7 — Photograph taken, 1909–1914, tied up to a mooring buoy in an unknown harbor along the East Coast of the United States. (Official U.S. Navy Photo)

Nevada (BM-8)

NAME (HULL NO.)	BUILDER	KEEL LAID	LAUNCHED	COMMISSIONED
NEVADA (BM-8)	Bath Iron	17 Apr 1899	24 Nov 1900	5 Mar 1903

Authorized 4 May 1898. Contract awarded 19 Oct 1898. Sponsored by Miss Grace Boutelle. First Commanding Officer: CDR Thomas B. Howard. Originally named CONNECTICUT. Renamed NEVADA January 1901. Rated as MONITOR NO. 8. Placed in comm., in reserve, 22 Oct 1906 at Annapolis, MD. Placed in full comm. 4 Jun 1907. Placed in comm., in reserve, 29 Aug 1907 at Annapolis, MD. Placed in full comm. 1 Jun 1908. Placed in comm., in reserve, 1 Sep 1908 at Annapolis, MD. Renamed TONOPAH 2 Mar 1909. Placed in full comm. 14 May 1909. Placed in comm., in reserve, 28 Jun 1909 at Annapolis, MD. Placed in ordinary 9 Nov 1915 at New London, CT. Decomm. 21 Oct 1919 at Philadelphia, PA. Classified BM-8 on 17 Jul 1920. Sold 26 Jan 1922 to Mr. Joseph G. Hitner & Mr. William F. Cutler, Philadelphia, PA. Scrapped.

Tonopah BM-8 — Photograph taken, 21 December 1917, tied up to a pier at the Boston Navy Yard, Boston, MA, with an early L-boat tied up alongside. Note that she wore a Mackay type camouflage. (Official U.S. Navy Photo)

NAME (HULL NO.)	BUILDER	KEEL LAID	LAUNCHED	COMMISSIONED
FLORIDA (BM-9)	Lewis Nixon	23 Jan 1899	30 Nov 1901	18 Jun 1903

Authorized 4 May 1898. Contract awarded 11 Oct 1898. Sponsored by Miss Sally Wood. First Commanding Officer: CDR John C. Fremont. Rated as MONITOR NO. 9. Placed in comm., in reserve, 11 Sep 1906 at Annapolis, MD. Placed in full comm. 4 Jun 1907. Placed in comm., in reserve, 30 Aug 1907 at Annapolis, MD. Decomm. 6 Jan 1908 at Norfolk, VA. Recomm. 21 May 1908. Decomm. 19 Jun 1908 at Norfolk, VA. Renamed TALLAHASSEE 20 Jun 1908. Placed in comm., in reserve, 1 Aug 1910. Classified BM-9 on 17 Jul 1920. Served as a reserve training ship from 3 Sep 1920 until March 1922 operating out of Charleston, SC. Reclass. UNCLASSIFIED VESSEL, IX-16 on 17 Jul 1921. Placed out of comm. 24 Mar 1922 at Philadelphia, PA. Struck 16 Jan 1922 from the NVR. Sold 25 Jul 1922 to the Ammunition Products Corp., Washington, DC, for $15,300.00. Scrapped.

Florida BM-9 — Photograph taken, 1905, while underway at an unknown location along the East Coast of the United States. (Official U.S. Navy Photo)

Florida BM-9 — Photograph taken, 1903–1908, anchored in an unknown harbor along the East Coast of the United States. (Official U.S. Navy Photo)

Tallahassee BM-9 — Photograph taken, 10 December 1916, anchored in Hampton Roads, VA. She is being used as a submarine tender with submarines K-5 (SS-36) and K-6 (SS-37) tied up alongside. (Ray D. Bean photo collection)

Wyoming (BM-10)

NAME (HULL NO.)	BUILDER	KEEL LAID	LAUNCHED	COMMISSIONED
WYOMING (BM-10)	Union Iron	11 Apr 1899	8 Sep 1900	8 Dec 1902

Authorized 4 May 1898. Contract awarded 5 Oct 1898. Sponsored by Miss Hattie Warren. First Commanding Officer: CDR Vincendon L. Cottman. Rated as MONITOR NO. 10. Decomm. 29 Aug 1905 at Vallejo, CA. Recomm. 8 Oct 1908. Renamed CHEYENNE 1 Jan 1909. Placed in comm., in reserve, 8 Jun 1909 at Vallejo, CA. Decomm. 13 Nov 1909 at Vallejo, CA. Placed in comm., in reserve, 11 Jul 1910. Decomm. 8 Feb 1913 for conversion to a submarine tender at Bremerton, WA. Recomm. 20 Aug 1913. Decomm. 4 Jan 1920 at Philadelphia, PA. Classified BM-10 on 17 Jul 1920. Recomm. 22 Sep 1920. Reclass. UNCLASSIFIED VESSEL, IX-4 on 17 Jul 1921. Served as a Naval Reserve training ship from October 1920 until 21 Jan 1926 operating out of Baltimore, MD. Decomm. 1 Jun 1926 at Philadelphia, PA. Struck 25 Jan 1937 from the NVR. Sold 20 Apr 1939 to the Boston Iron & Metal Co., Baltimore, MD, for $37,000.00. Scrapped.

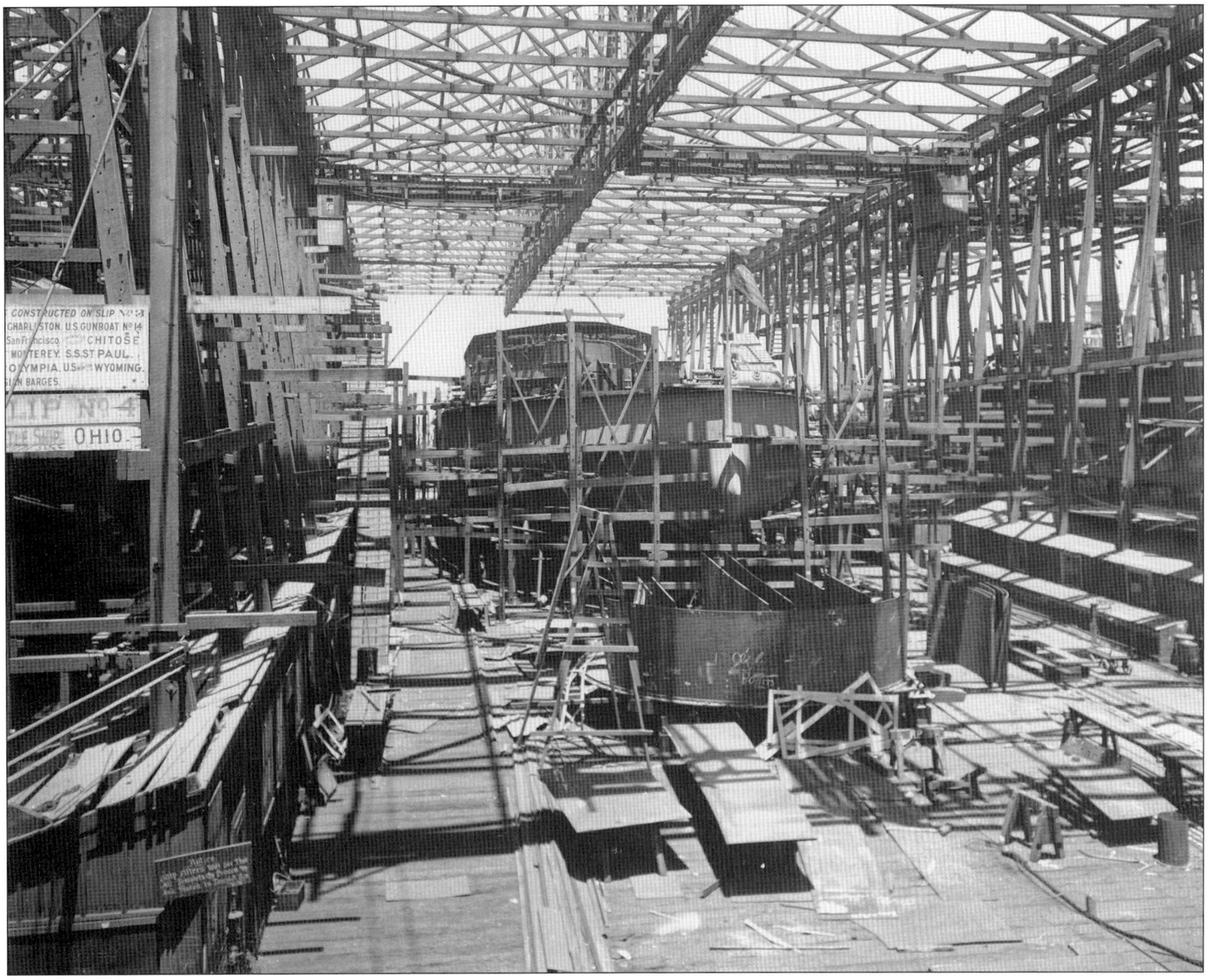

Wyoming BM-10 — Photograph taken, 30 June 1900, while under construction on the slipway looking at the bow at the Union Iron Works, San Francisco, CA. (Official U.S. Navy Photo)

Wyoming BM-10 — Photograph taken, February 1903, anchored off of the Mare Island Navy Yard, Vallejo, CA. (Ray D. Bean photo collection)

Class Specifications			As Completed (1902/1903)
HULL	LENGTH	Waterline	252' 0"
		Overall	255' 1"
	EXTREME BEAM		50' 0"
	DISPLACEMENT	Full Load	3,356 tons
		Normal	3,225 tons
	MEAN DRAFT		12' 6"
	COMPLEMENT	Officers	13
		Enlisted	209
ARMAMENT		Main	(1) twin 12"/40 B.L.R. turret
		Secondary	(4) single 4"/50 R.F. mounts
			(3) single 6 pdr.
	ARMOR	Belt	
		Top	11"
		Bottom	5"
		Waterline	8"
		Deck	1.5"
		Turrets	9" – 10"
		Barbettes	9" – 11"
		Conning Tower	8"
ENGINEERING	SPEED	Maximum	12.0 knots (BM-7)
			13.0 knots (BM-8)
			12.4 knots (BM-9)
			11.8 knots (BM-10)
		Economical	10.0 knots
	ENGINES	Manufacturer	Newport News (BM-7)
			Bath (BM-8)
			Lewis Nixon (BM-9)
			Union (BM-10)
		Type	Vert. 3-Exp. Recip.
	HORSEPOWER	Indicated	1,830 (BM-7)
			2,004 (BM-8)
			2,395 (BM-9)
			2,452 (BM-10)
	SCREWS		2
	BOILERS	Manufacturer	Newport News (BM-7)
			Niclausse (BM-8)
			Lewis Nixon (BM-9)
			B & W (BM-10)
		Type/No.	Thornycroft WT/4 (BM-7)
			WT/4 (BM-8, 10)
			Mosher WT/4 (BM-9)
	FUEL CAPACITY		344 tons coal (BM-7, 10)
			338 tons coal (BM-8)
			355 tons coal (BM-9)

Bibliography

A. Official

Naval Vessels Register (NAVSHIPS 18-1-1), Jan. 1946. Government Printing Office, Washington, DC
Naval Vessels Register (NAVSHIPS 18-1-4), July 1946. Government Printing Office, Washington, DC
Naval Vessels Register (NAVSHIPS 18-1-7), Apr. 1947. Government Printing Office, Washington, DC
Naval Vessels Register (NAVSHIPS 18-1-9), Jan. 1948. Government Printing Office, Washington, DC
Naval Vessels Register (NAVSHIPS 18-1-13), Jan. 1950. Government Printing Office, Washington, DC
Naval Vessels Register (NAVSHIPS 18-1-16), Jan. 1950. Government Printing Office,Washington, DC
Naval Vessels Register (NAVSHIPS 18-1-19), Jan. 1953. Government Printing Office, Washington, DC
Naval Vessels Register (NAVSHIPS 18-1-25), July 1956. Government Printing Office, Washington, DC
Naval Vessels Register/Ships Data Book (NAVSHIPS 250-574-8), Government Printing Office, Washington, DC; editions of Vol I, Jan. 1964, Vol I, Jan. 1965,
Vol I, Jan. 1969, Vol I, Jan. 1976, Vol I, Jan. 1978, Vol I, Jan. 1980, Vol I, Jan. 1982,
Vol I, Jan. 1984, Vol I, Jan. 1986, Vol I, Jan. 1988, Vol I, Jan. 1990, Vol I, Jan. 1992,
Vol I, Jan. 1993.
Report of the Secretary of the Navy, 1892, Government Printing Office, Washington, DC
Ships Data U.S. Naval Vessels, Government Printing Office, Washington, DC; editions of 1911, 1912, 1914, 1916, 1917, Feb. 1918, Nov. 1918, 1919, 1920, 1921, 1922, 1924, 1929, 1931, 1935 and 1938.
Ships Data U.S. Naval Vessels, (Ships 8)1943, Government Printing Office, Washington, DC
Ships Data U.S. Naval Vessels, Vol I (NAVSHIPS 250-010)1945, Government Printing Office, Washington, DC; editions of Vol I, Vol II and Vol III.
United States Maritime Commission, Construction Division, Permanent Report of Completed Ship Construction Contracts, Report B-1, Washington, DC, Aug. 1945.
United States Navy, BuOrd Vessels Register, Government Printing Office, Washington, DC; editions of March 25, 1945, May 25, 1945, September 25, 1945 and November 25, 1945.
United States Navy, Chief of Naval Operations, Naval History Division.
A. Ships History Section data files
B. Operational Archives "Records of the General Board"
C. Miscellaneous Records

B. Unofficial

Friedman, Norman. *U.S. Battleships*. Naval Institute Press, Annapolis, MD, 1985
Benham, Edith W, and Hall, Anne M. *Ships of the United States Navy and Their Sponsors*. Plimpton Press, Norwood, Mass., 1913
Benham, Edith W, and Hall, Anne M. *Ships of the United States Navy and Their Sponsors*. Plimpton Press, Norwood, Mass., 1915
Rowe, John S, and Morison, Samuel L. *Encyclopedia of Major United States Warships (1900-1978)*. Unpublished manuscript in possession of the author.
Somerville, Keith Frazier, and Smith, Harriotte W.B. *Ships of the United States Navy and Their Sponsors, 1924-1950*. United States Naval Institute, Annapolis, MD., 1952.

C. Websites

DANFS – Dictionary of American Naval Fighting Ships. Contains ship histories on most U.S. Navy ships. www.history.navy.mil
Usndazzle – Contains a great deal of information about camouflage and camouflage patterns used on U.S. Navy ships during WWII. www.usndazzle.com
NavSource – Contains photographs and brief histories of U.S. Navy ships. www.navsource.org
Ship Camouflage – Contains an online database of camouflage used by U.S. Navy ships during WWII. www.shipcamouflage.com

Camouflage

Measure 1	Dark Gray (5-D) overhaul except for Light Gray (5-L) structures above the stack tops. Steel horizontal surfaces were Dark Gray; wooden decks were left bare, except for aircraft carriers which continued to use Mahogany Red stain on flight decks. Measure 1 was to be the default paint scheme for the entire Navy in the absence of other instructions.
Measure 5	A painted white bow wave used in combination with Measure 1, 2 or 3 to give the impression of high speed at all times.
Measure 12 Modified	Sea Blue on the hull up to the main deck (hanger deck on aircraft carriers), Ocean Gray from main deck level to the top of the superstructure masses, and Haze Gray (5-H) for masts and other vertical projections above superstructure level. Horizontal surfaces painted Deck Blue. Canvas dyed blue. In Measure 12 (Modified), irregular patches or splotches were added to break up the ship's profile: Haze Gray splotches on Sea Blue (later Navy Blue) and vice versa, and Sea Blue (later Navy Blue) splotches on Ocean Gray. "These splotches should be obtained by extending the Navy Blue paint into the designated Ocean Gray paint area and vice versa. They should be about 1/3 the area of a rectangle 12 feet high by 20 feet long." There were no specific instructions on the positioning or shape of the splotches, which were left up to individual captains, yards or maintenance facilities, and the recommended size was frequently disregarded, so that no two ships look alike. Measure 12 (Mod) was used extensively in both fleets during 1942. Unfortunately the splotches in most cases were too small to break up the ship's outline effectively, and at any distance resolved into simple gray.
Measure 14	Ocean Gray overall. "Useful for protection against submarine attack, where aerial observation is a lesser factor. In Atlantic or Pacific Coastal waters where weather is generally sunny, visibility is high, and bright moonlight is common at night."
Measure 21	Overall Navy Blue (5-N), with decks in dark Deck Blue (20-B). This measure was used extensively in the western and southern Pacific from September 1942 through 1945 to minimize detection and identification by enemy aircraft.
Measure 22	Navy Blue (5-N) low on the hull below the first continuous deck, with Haze Gray (5-H) above that. Measure 22 used a straight horizontal boundary between the two colors rather than following the sheer of the main deck, making a characteristic gray "wedge" at the bow. This bold contrast at a horizontal line near the horizon reduced visibility to surface observers and created the illusion of greater range.
Measure 31 (Disruptive system, dark)	Dark pattern Measure 31 was a series of irregular geometric patterns using large polygonal and striped patterns of Black and Ocean Gray, or Black, Ocean Gray and Haze Gray. The patterns and tones were designed to resolve at a distance to an average low reflectivity of 10–20%. Horizontal surfaces also carried irregular patterns in Ocean Gray and Deck Blue. This measure emphasized mistaken identity and course deception to complicate submarine attack. Patterns were carried across the bow, and light gray was used aft to blend with the wake. Undersides of horizontal elements were countershaded in Pale Gray (5-P) or White (5-U) to reduce self-shadowing. In 1944 revised Measure 31a substituted Navy Blue for Black and eliminated counter-shading.
Measure 32 (Disruptive system, medium)	Medium pattern Measure 32 was similar to Measure 31 but somewhat lighter, a mixture of obtrusive polygons in Black against background polygons of Light Gray, or Light Gray and Ocean Gray. The patterns and tones were designed to resolve as a distance to an average medium reflectivity of 20–30%. Measure 32 was applied to most surface ships in the Pacific during 1944, but in 1945 the Pacific Fleet reverted to Measure 12, 21, or 22 in the revised 1945 colors.

Camouflage Design Sheets

31a/6B	BB-36	
31a/7B	BB-33	
31a/8B	BB-34	
32/1D	BB-43	
32/6D	BB-40, BB-41	
32/7D	BB-48	
32/16D	BB-44	
32/18D (Early)	BB-55	
32/18D (Late)	BB-55	Sheet not available
32/22D	BB-63	
32a/1B	BB-61	Sheet not available

Note: Some data sheets are in poor condition and maybe difficult to read.

Camouflage Measure 31a, Design 6B, for USS Nevada (BB-36) – port side

Camouflage Measure 31a, Design 6B, for USS Nevada (BB-36) – starboard side

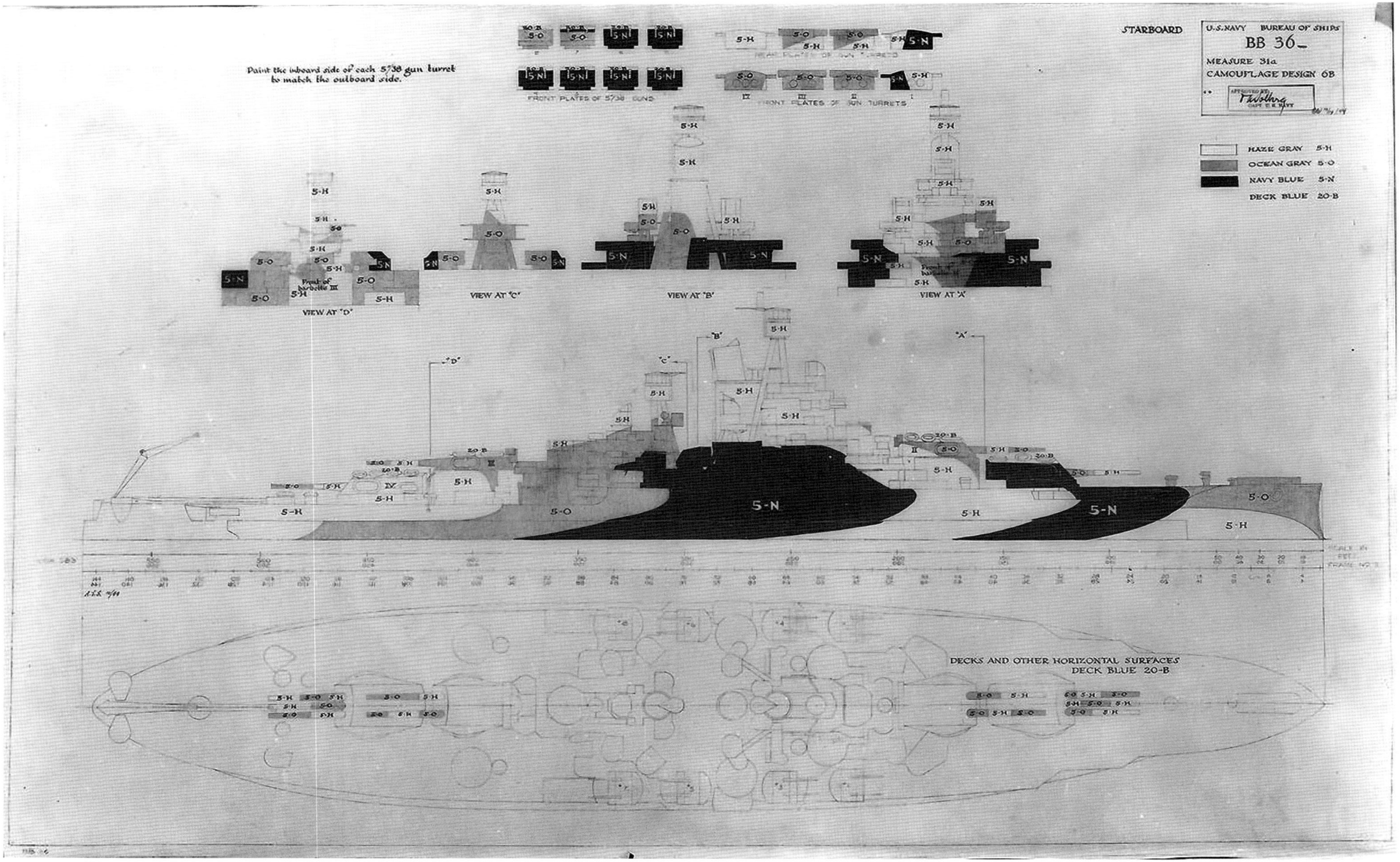

Camouflage Measure 31a, Design 7B, for USS Arkansas (BB-33) – port side

Camouflage Measure 31a, Design 7B, for USS Arkansas (BB-33) – starboard side

Camouflage Measure 31a, Design 8B, for USS New York (BB-34) – port side

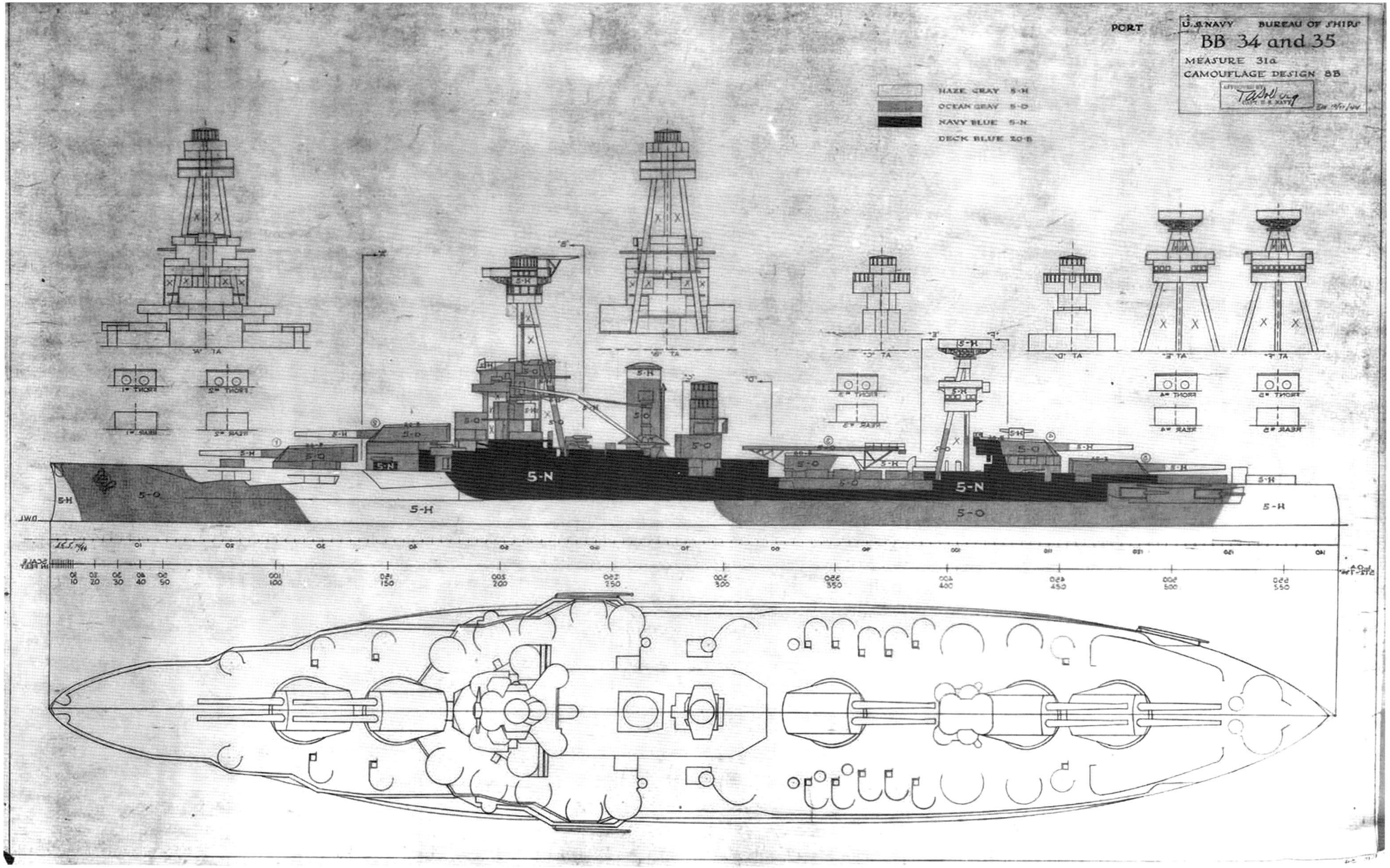

Camouflage Measure 31a, Design 8B, for USS New York (BB-34) – starboard side

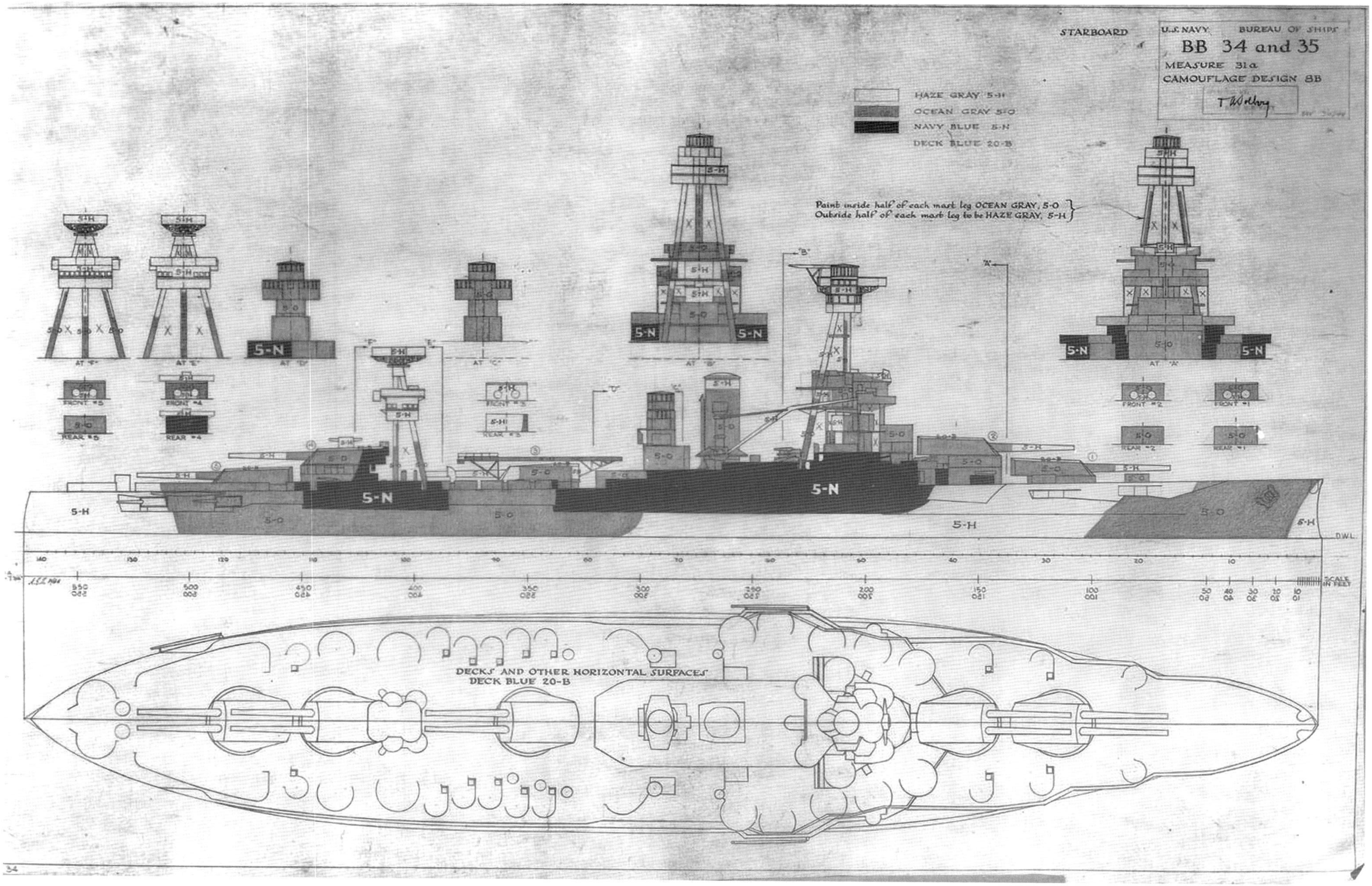

Camouflage Measure 32, Design 1D, for USS Tennessee (BB-43) – port side

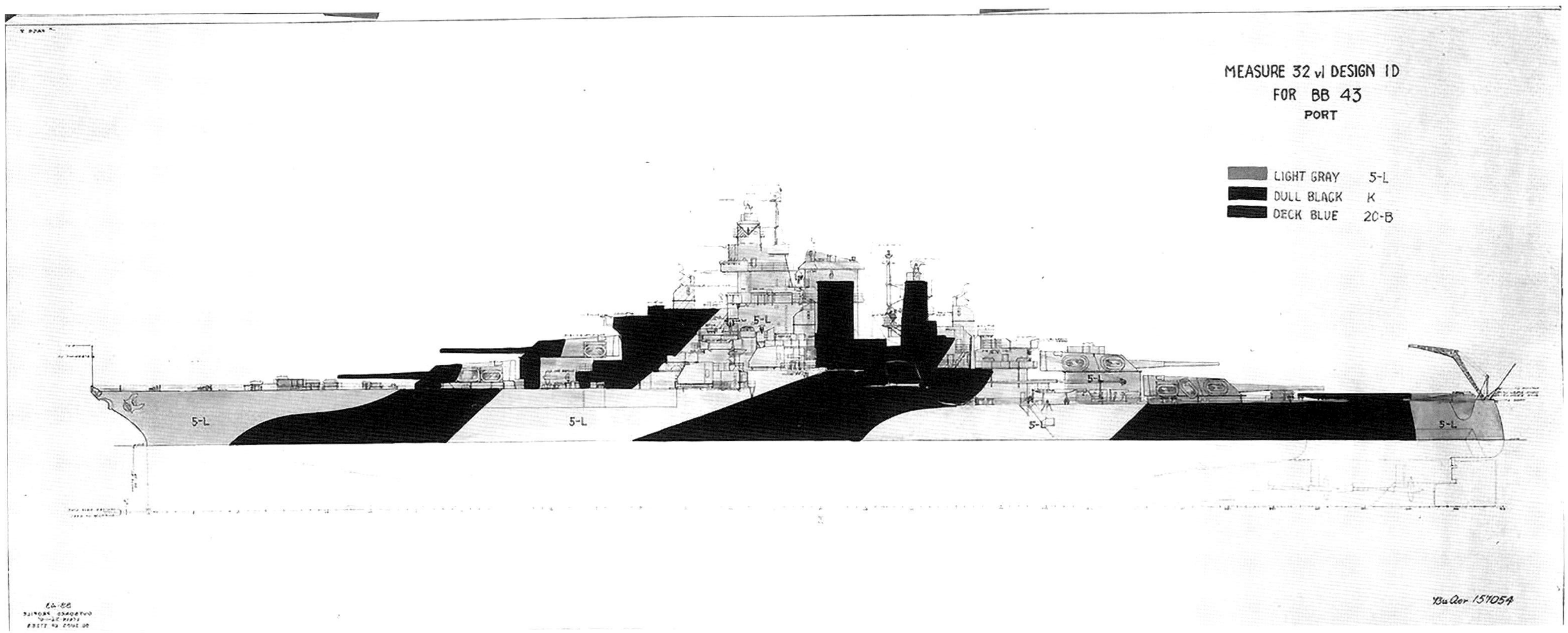

Camouflage Measure 32, Design 1D, for USS Tennessee (BB-43) – starboard side

Camouflage Measure 32, Design 6D, for USS New Mexico (BB-40) and USS Mississippi (BB-41) – port side

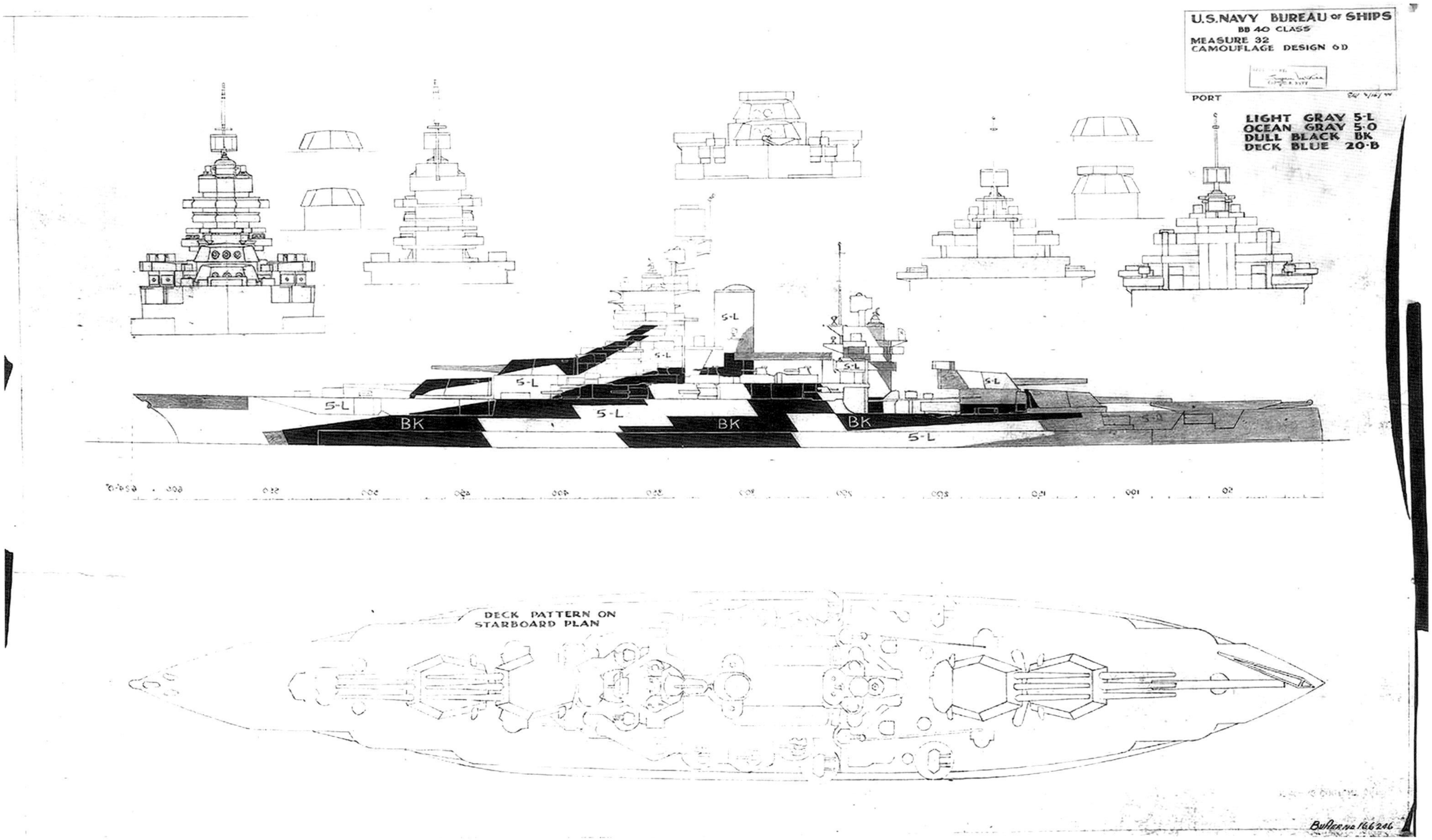

Camouflage Measure 32, Design 6D, for USS New Mexico (BB-40) and USS Mississippi (BB-41) – starboard side

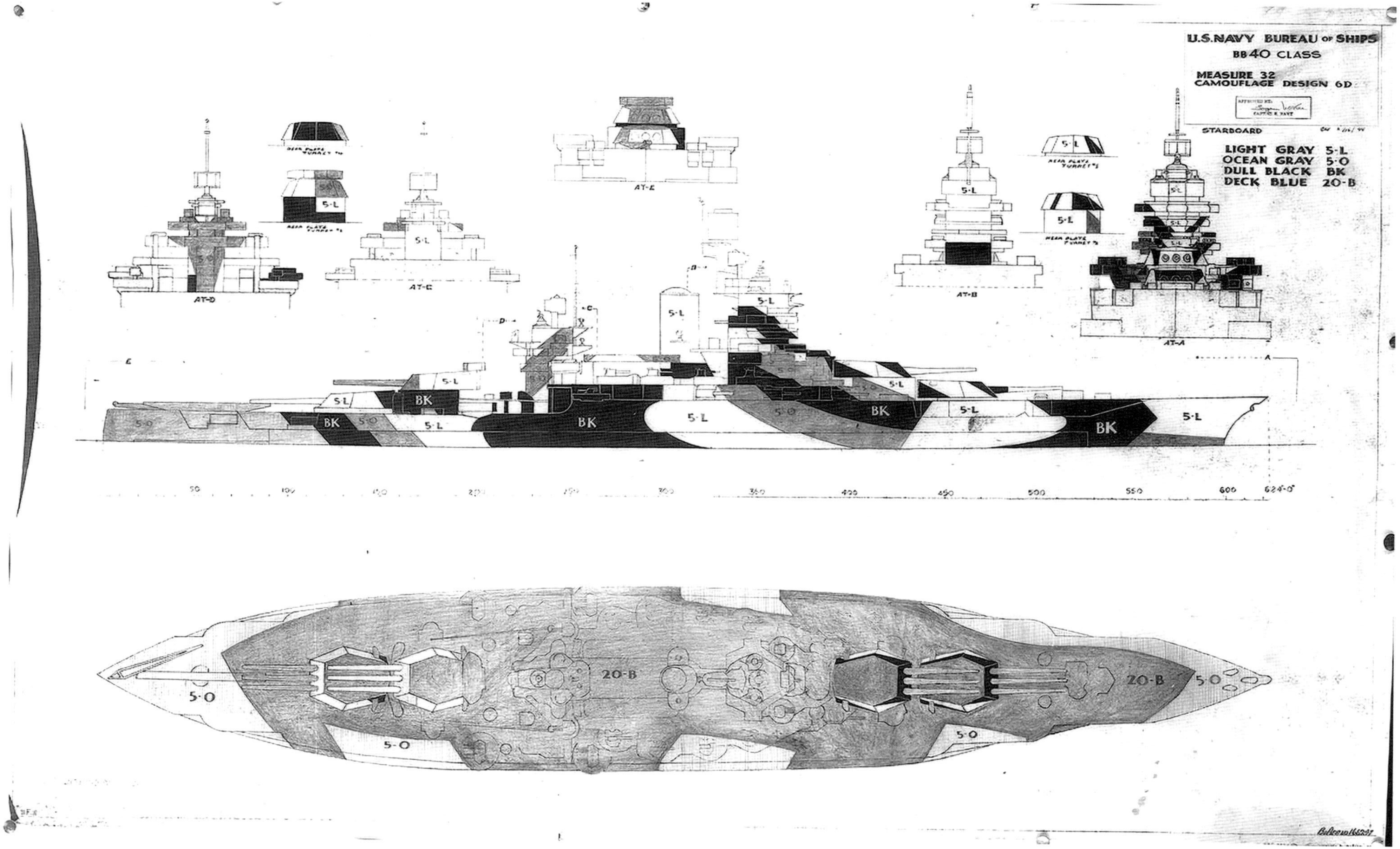

Camouflage Measure 32, Design 7D, for USS West Virginia (BB-48) – port side

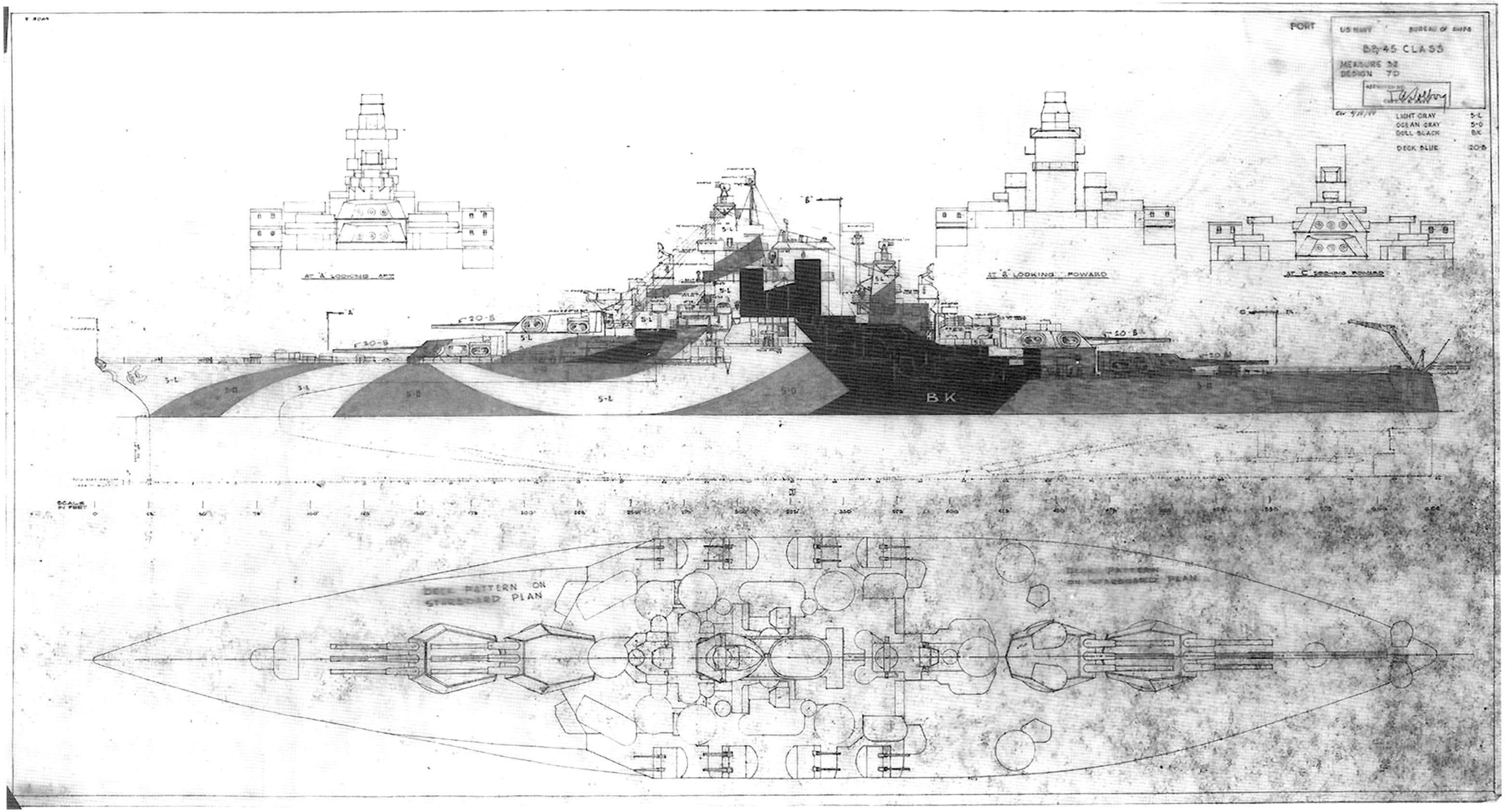

Camouflage Measure 32, Design 7D, for USS West Virginia (BB-48) – starboard side

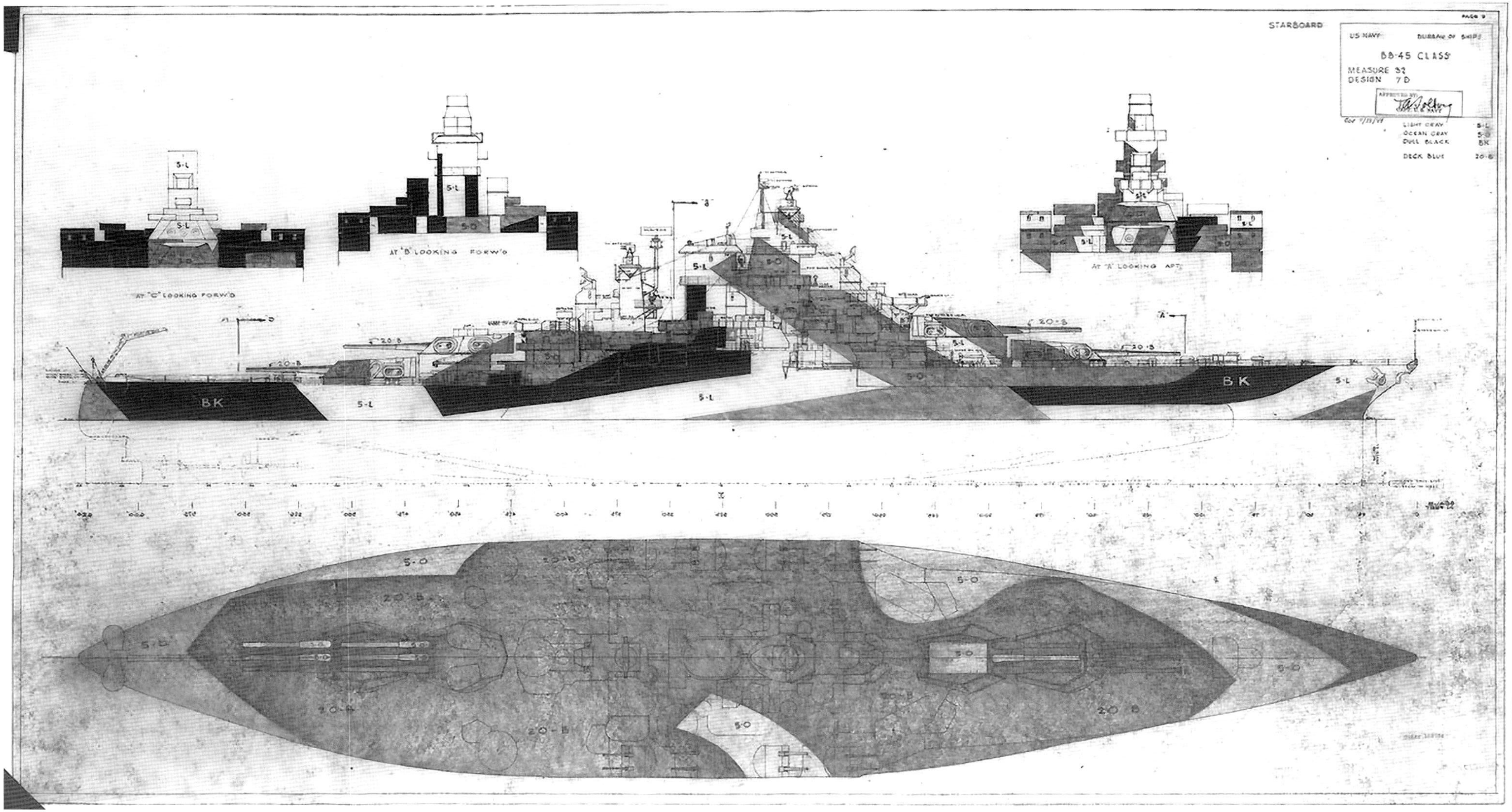

Camouflage Measure 32, Design 16D, for USS California (BB-44) – port side

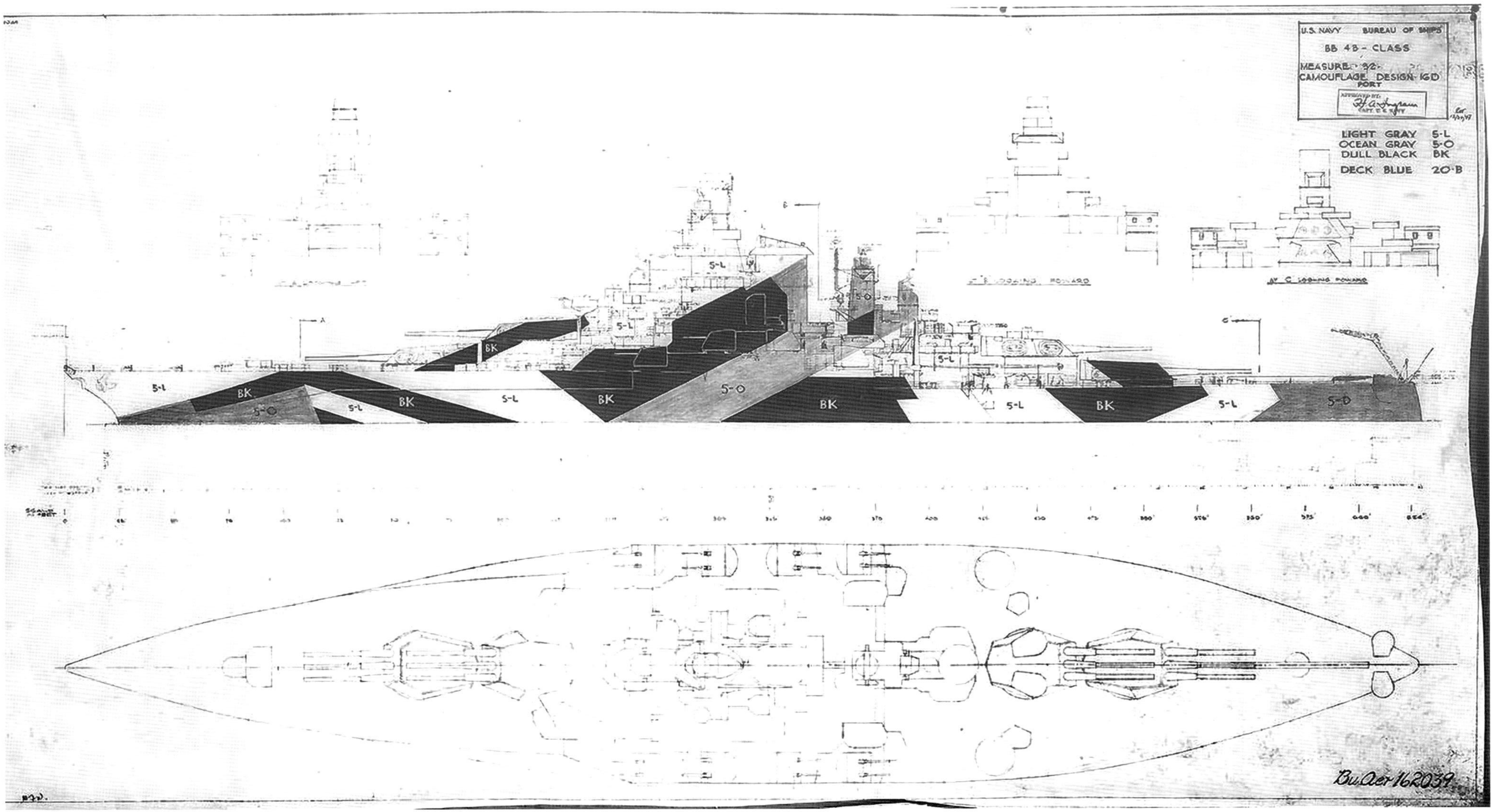

Camouflage Measure 32, Design 16D, for USS California (BB-44) – starboard side

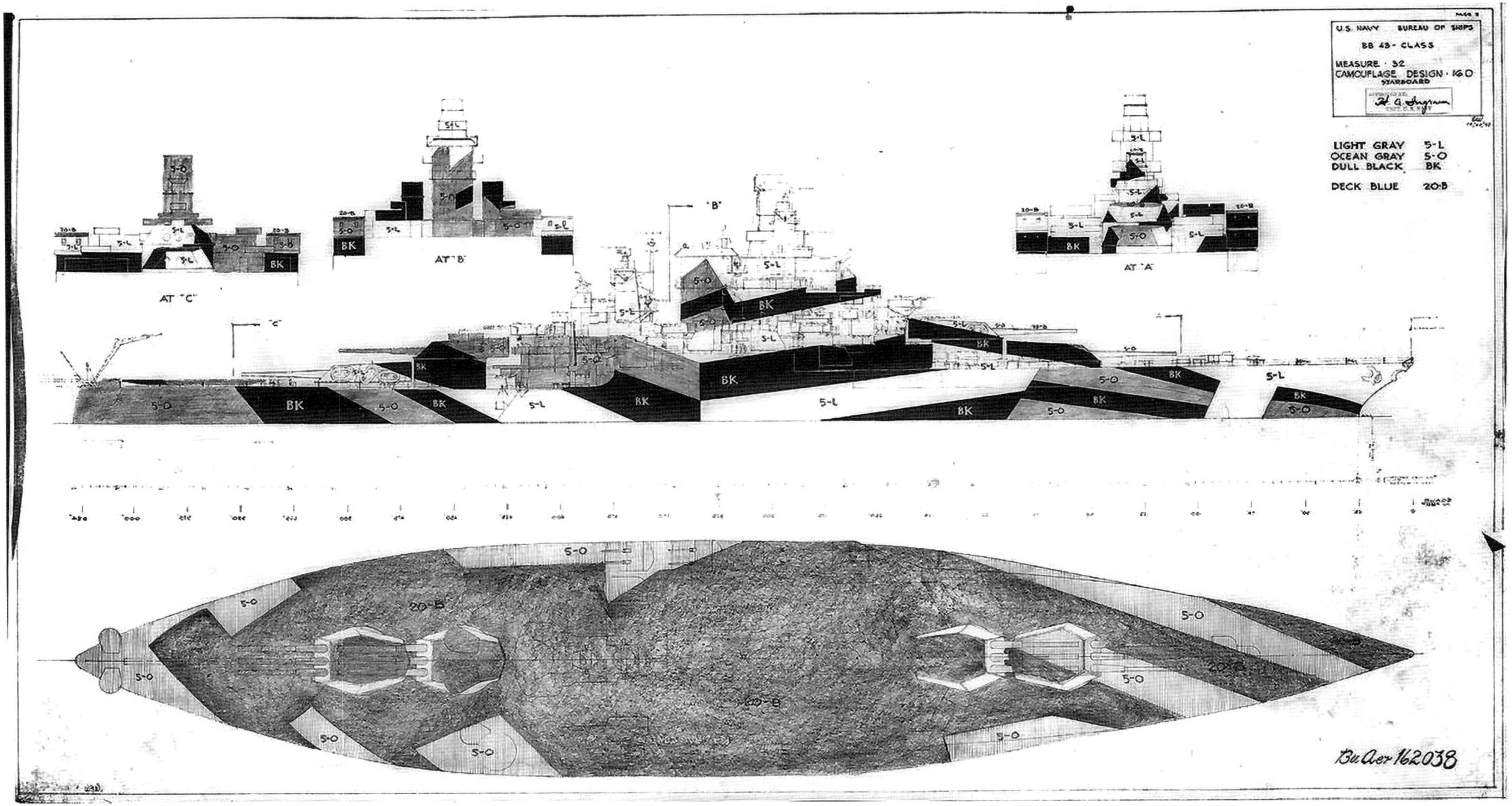

Camouflage Measure 32, Design 18D (Early), for USS North Carolina (BB-55) – port side

Camouflage Measure 32, Design 18D (Early), for USS North Carolina (BB-55) – starboard side

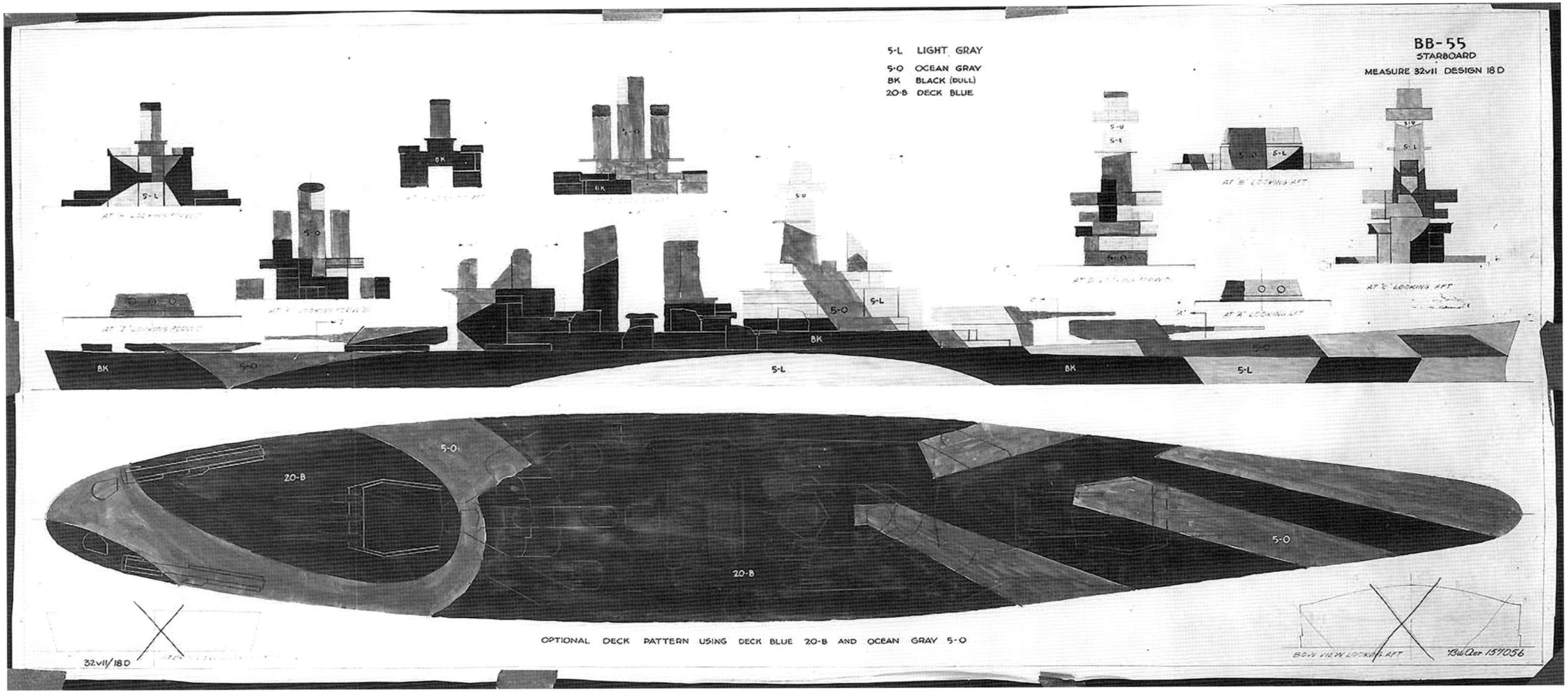

Camouflage Measure 32, Design 22D, for USS Missouri (BB-63) – port side

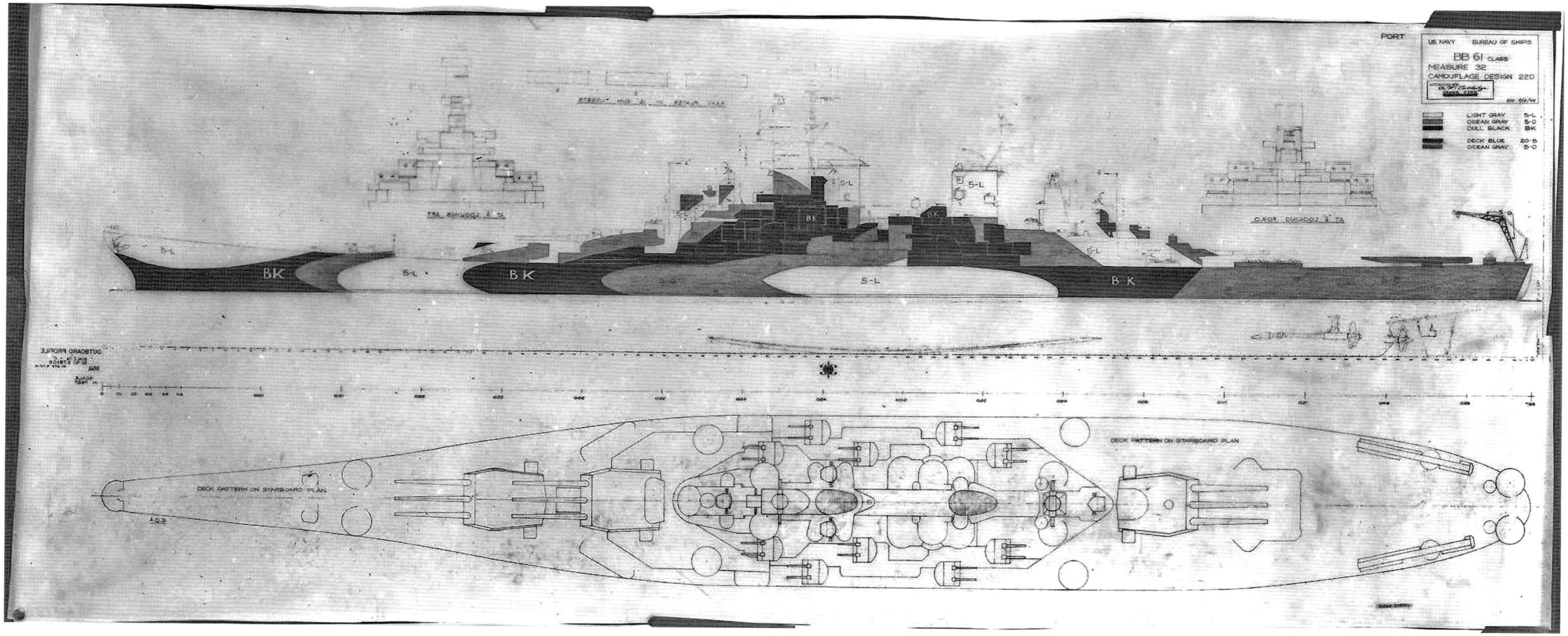

Camouflage Measure 32, Design 22D, for USS Missouri (BB-63) – starboard side

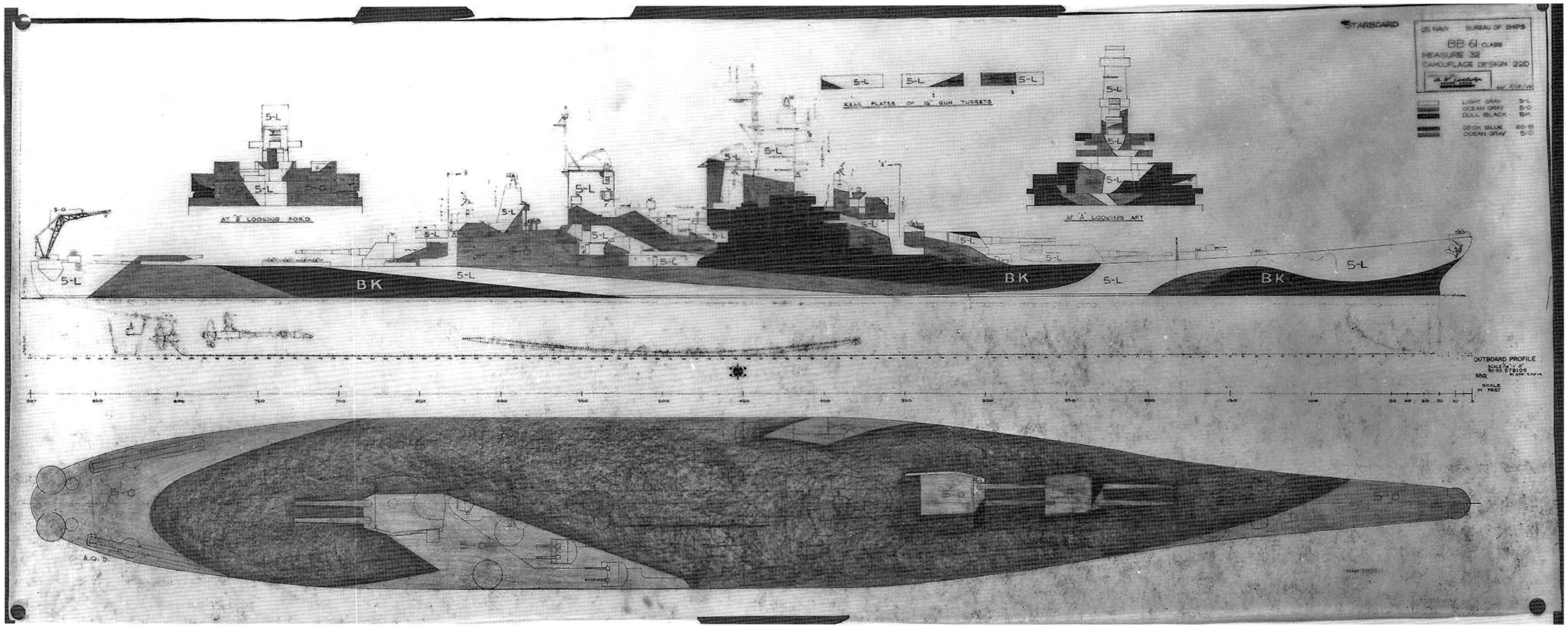

Ship Name Index